Becoming Israeli

THE HYSTERICAL, INSPIRING AND

CHALLENGING SIDES OF MAKING ALIYAH

Becoming Israeli

The Hysterical, Inspiring and Challenging Sides of Making Aliyah

EDITED BY

Akiva Gersh

RIMONIM PRESS

Typeset by Raphaël Freeman, Renana Typesetting
Cover design by The Virtual Paintbrush

ISBN: 978-0-692-89988-5

Contents

SETTLING IN

BECOMING BILINGUAL (OR AT LEAST TRYING!)

ISRAELIFYING

To the land of Israel.
For never doubting that we would return home.

Acknowledgments

I feel deep gratitude to many people who came together in different ways to help make this book a reality.

First and foremost, to the writers found in the pages of this book. It goes without saying that without all of them, this book would not exist. But more than that, their words have inspired me tremendously, and my hope is that many others will also be moved by reading their personal tales of aliyah, tales which are filled with passion, inspiration, courage, determination, and strength.

An enormous thank you to Yossi Klein Halevi for all of the advice and guidance he shared with me throughout the entire process of bringing this book to life. It was humbling to have such an accomplished writer, one for whom I personally have great respect and admiration, assist me along this journey with his endless patience and abundant insight and wisdom.

Thank you to Miriam Herschlag, the Ops and Blogs editor at The Times of Israel, for her excitement and support of this book. The blog space she oversees has created an online forum where English-speaking olim can share, among other things, their aliyah stories and journeys in full color. As most of the blogs here originally appeared as TOI blogs, this book owes a great deal to this incredible community.

Thank you to Raphaël Freeman, whose vast knowledge and expertise greatly helped to shape this book. He was a constant source of advice and direction, always willing to help me understand the ins and outs of the world of publishing.

Thank you to Ariane Mandell, whose careful editing eye brought my book to an entirely new professional level. Above and beyond the technical changes she made to the text, her questions and suggestions on the content and style of the book helped me to think about things I would not have otherwise considered.

Thank you to Hadassa Field for her careful proofreading of the final version of the manuscript. Through her patience and skilled and watchful eyes, she brought the book to its finished form.

Thank you to Eliezer Shore, Stuart Schnee, and Sarah Tuttle-Singer, who indulged my many questions and always had the time to offer sound advice. Each of you, in your own way, made the process of publishing more understandable and much more navigable.

My deepest gratitude goes to my wife Tamar. You were not only the creative source for the final form of this book, you also gave me endless time and support throughout the long process of this work, from sharing in my excitement, to giving advice, to simply just listening to me, time and again, talk about the project. This book simply would not have come to be without you.

Finally, thank you to my kids, Shaiya, Noa, Ella, and Adiv, who, though they do not yet know, are the true inspiration for this book. Watching you be born and raised in Israel, our country and homeland, has been the biggest blessing of my life. I bless you that you should always be aware of the miracle and the importance of the Jewish state, and do your part in keeping it safe, strong, and, most importantly, a light unto the nations.

Introduction

AKIVA GERSH

When I made aliyah, it was euphoric.

I had brought my acoustic guitar on the plane with me to make sure it didn't get damaged with the cargo. As my wife, Tamar, and I were beginning to descend the stairs to the tarmac below, the thought suddenly entered my mind to take my guitar out of its case and play a song for this overwhelming once-in-a-lifetime moment. I took out my guitar and, without any conscious thought as to what song to sing, "Am Yisrael Chai" burst from my lips. More than that, it burst forth from deep in my soul.

There I was, arriving in Israel as I had many times before, but this time not merely to visit, not only for my annual recharge that would give me the strength to live another year outside of Israel. This time, I was coming to live *for the rest of my life*. To plant my roots in the land. To change the course not only of my life but of my future children's lives as well, and their children's and their children's. To be part of the greatest and most miraculous migration the world has ever seen.

I had no return ticket home. This time, a one-way ticket was all I needed to take me home.

I landed at the bottom of the stairs and continued to strum and to sing as I walked between two rows of IDF soldiers who had come to celebrate with us. Their smiling mouths opened up and began to sing with me. Our voices joined together in what, for me, was 2000 years of Jewish history declaring loud and proud: *Am Yisrael Chai*. The people of Israel live.

That was 2004. Since then, there have been many other euphoric moments living in Israel as well as emotional and inspiring moments. At the Kotel praying with thousands of other people, viscerally feeling what it's like to be part of a nation standing together. Hearing *Eichah* on Tisha B'Av with a small group of battle-tired soldiers on the Gaza border during Operation Protective Edge. Hiking in the Negev in the middle of the night with only the full moon to illuminate the ancient desert floor. Crawling through 2000-year-old caves with my students, teaching them about Jewish strength and pride. And so many more.

But there also have been many other kinds of moments. Frustrating moments, like trying to explain to the Jerusalem Municipality that I didn't mean to not pay my *arnona* (housing tax) for three years, I just didn't know that I had to, and therefore they should cancel the 5000 shekel fine they gave me. Which they didn't. Complicated moments, like watching my children go off to *gan* (nursery school) even though they still didn't fully understand Hebrew. Scary moments, like moving my sleeping children into our protected room during an air-raid siren because of rockets coming toward our town from the Gaza Strip.

Living in Israel has been anything but stagnant, anything but monotonous. From walking in the middle of car-free streets on Yom Kippur, to delivering pizzas to soldiers on the Gaza border, to making embarrassing mistakes in Hebrew, to watching my 5-year-old son stand up during a nation-wide siren to remember Israel's fallen soldiers and thinking to myself, "He's only five years old, and he already gets it." The powerful and complex moments that I have in one month in Israel would take years to occur anywhere else in the world.

Coming to Israel made me a citizen of the first independent Jewish state in over 2000 years. It also made me an immigrant, something I never thought in my life I would be, something I somehow didn't realize I would become upon making aliyah. It forced me to reflect upon my own grandparents' immigrant experience. They left Poland for America in the late 1930s, a decision that, most importantly, saved their lives, but also forever made them foreigners in a country that to me, was simply home. As a kid, I didn't fully understand my grandparents and, at times, was even embarrassed that they spoke differently, dressed differently, and acted differently from my friends' fully American grandparents. Now, I was the one speaking differently, dressing differently, and acting differently. Trying to find my way and make my way in a country that wasn't supposed to be foreign (this is the Jewish state after all, right?). But, in reality, it partially was. I was simultaneously fulfilling my greatest dream of coming home to Israel and, at the same time, living on a different planet. At the very least in a very different culture. I had spiritual memories of this place, memories from time immemorial, yet I was unfamiliar with many of the cultural norms that made Israel Israel.

It's been 13 years since the day I sang "Am Yisrael Chai" with those soldiers in that moment of euphoric bliss. I've had the full range of all kinds of other moments ever since. Moments that have made me wonder why my wife and I didn't go west instead of east and move to Northern California, and moments that have broken my heart with the deep realization of never having done anything in my life as incredible and as important as moving to Israel.

This book is a reflection of those moments. It is a collection of blogs and essays written by over 40 English-speaking olim (immigrants), that together give an inside look into the never-ending joys and challenges, inspirations and frustrations that we have experienced along our journeys of aliyah. It is also, in my humble opinion, a peek into one of humanity's most incredible stories – the story of the Jewish people returning home.

Foreword: Coming Home

YOSSI KLEIN HALEVI

Summer 2017 marks 35 years since I left New York City and moved to Israel. I've now been here for half the life of the state, and more than half of my life.

Summer 1982 was a terrible moment in Israel's history. It was the time of the First Lebanon War (which we simply called the Lebanon War, because we didn't know there would be a second). It was a hard time to be joining Israeli society. Not just because Israel was at war, but because Israel was at war with itself. Until then, war had always united Israelis; now, it was dividing them. People shouted at each other on street corners – Traitors! Warmongers! Entire units of reservists, after being demobilized from front-line duty, would head directly to the Prime Minister's office in Jerusalem to protest the war. A few weeks after I landed, the Sabra and Shatila massacre occurred, and Israel became a pariah. That first Rosh Hashanah, I saw Prime Minister Menachem Begin walking out of the Great Synagogue in Jerusalem, as Peace Now demonstrators shouted at him, "Murderer!"

Everyone seemed to be asking me: Why? Why leave the safest and most prosperous refuge Jews have ever known for one of the most dangerous places to be a Jew? Why abandon a country where the great threat to Jewish survival is an excess of non-Jewish love for an uncertain home in the Middle East, where Jews are as hated as we have ever been, anywhere, at any time? And why bring children – in my case then, future children – into an environment where they would be required to defend their country?

Perhaps most painfully, the "why" question wasn't only asked by friends and family I left behind but by some of my new fellow Israelis. Why would you leave the country I'm dying to get into, some said to me, and come here of all places? Didn't you have it good in America? Surely, went the unspoken subtext, there must be something wrong with this misfit who couldn't find his place in the greatest country in history.

Eventually, I came to appreciate those encounters with perplexed Israelis as an essential part of my absorption process, exchanging romantic Zionism for the hard privilege of belonging to the real Israel.

The question, "why?" runs through the intensely personal reflections in this book. Why a Jew from America or England or Australia would move to Israel – to the Middle East – is, in fact, a reasonable question. That's especially true for the contributors of this volume, many of whom came here around the time of the Second Intifada of the early 2000s, when the hope of the peace process ended in exploding buses and Israel entered the worst time in its history – the ongoing war against the home front, which has continued, in one form or another, ever since the Second Intifada, shifting from one part of the country to another. They came, in other words, to an Israel that no longer believed in the possibility of peace – a sense that has only deepened as the Middle East disintegrates.

My response to "why" has changed over the years. I came here as a journalist, and offered a journalist's answer to that question. I made aliyah, I would say in my first years here, because I wanted to know the Israeli story in its fullness – not only the headlines but the "back pages" of Israeli life.

When my children began showing up, I offered a different

answer. The *sevivonim* – "dreidels" – on which I grew up in America, I explained to them every Hanukkah, were imprinted with the Hebrew letters representing the words, "A great miracle happened there." The *sevivonim* in Israel, I continued, replaced the letter representing "there" with the letter for "here." And so I moved to Israel because I wanted to be in the country of "here," not "there." I stopped repeating that story when they started rolling their eyes. But they got the point: The main plot of the Jewish story was once again being written *here*.

Sometimes, I answered the "why" question by saying that I came home to join the totality of the Jewish people. In the Diaspora, Jews function as communities, not a people. A community is a self-selecting entity, and often reflects ideological and social homogeneity. Living in the Diaspora, you can avoid those Jews whose ideas or way of life you find abhorrent. In Israel, we are deprived of that option, because here we are a people, coerced into intimacy with our maddening, vitalizing diversity.

I once asked an immigrant from Moscow what had most surprised her about Israel. "The existence of stupid Jews," she said. In Moscow, she explained, all the Jews she knew were intelligent. How could there be stupid Jews in Israel? But then, one day, she understood: In Moscow Jews were a minority, and a minority always has to be better than the majority to be just as good. But here in Israel, Jews can be as smart or as stupid as they actually are.

That was another way of noting the difference between community and peoplehood.

Moving to Israel during the Lebanon War, at Israel's most divisive moment until that time, confronted me with a dilemma. How to enter a society that was tearing itself apart? Do I choose a camp – a tribe – and turn that into "my" Israel?

I opted for another route. If I'd really come to join the people of Israel, then choosing one tribe would deprive me of an affinity with others. And so I embraced Israeli society in all of its contradictions. Of course I make my political and cultural choices. But I refuse to identify with any one tribe to the exclusion of others. Israel's arguments over identity and borders and peace are being debated inside of me; I insist on the right to being a multi-dimensional Israeli.

In my early years here, like many enthusiastic olim, I would obnoxiously preach aliyah to Jews back in America. "How can you possibly live anywhere but here?" I demanded. I no longer believe that all Jews must live in Israel. I have come to cherish Diaspora as the essential counter-point to homeland, part of what has made us an "*am olam*" – a nation of the world, a nation of eternity.

Still, I admit that I am perplexed. How is it that Jews for whom Jewish identity is central to their lives don't come home? I've long since stopped judging – life is too complicated – but I do remain puzzled. How do they manage to keep away?

And that's another reason why I came: I couldn't keep away any longer. Even during a war. Especially during a war.

I once interviewed Israeli novelist David Grossman, who said that he receives numerous invitations for a sabbatical abroad, but that he's never taken any offers, because he doesn't want to deprive his children of a year of life in Israel. Too much happens here, there are too many changes to be away for an entire year. Where else could Grossman's children experience such vitality? (I thought of that story when Grossman's son, Uri, was killed in the Second Lebanon War in 2006.)

I know what he means. My family went abroad for a year – 1989–1990 – and when we returned, there were Russian musicians playing cello in the streets and Cyrillic letters on the dairy products in the supermarket. The Iron Curtain had opened that year, and tens of thousands, and soon hundreds of thousands, of lost Jews from the Soviet Union were landing at Ben-Gurion Airport. One year abroad, and I returned to a different country.

Sometimes, I tell friends visiting from America on their tenth or twentieth or fiftieth trip, that the reason I made aliyah is that I didn't want to waste my vacations on trips to Israel.

A confession: Every time I land at Ben-Gurion after a trip abroad, and head for the line earmarked for Israeli passport holders, I experience something of the thrill I felt as a new immigrant. I tell myself to stop being sentimental, but it doesn't work. I'm always grateful anew to be an Israeli returning home, no longer a tourist at the gates of Israel.

After all these years, after all the mistakes we've made here – and it sometimes seems that we're compensating for centuries of homelessness by repeating every possible mistake a sovereign nation can make – I still believe that this is the place. Not the *only* place for Jews, but the *ultimate* place. I still worry that when I go abroad I will miss something essential in the Israeli story. As the old Arik Einstein song put it, "*Zohi harpatkat hayenu*," this is the great adventure of our lives.

Today, after 35 years, I'm rarely confronted anymore with the "why" question. Instead, well-intentioned visitors from abroad sometimes ask whether I "like it" here. I reply that there are aspects of Israeli life that I like very much – my wife, Sarah, and I used to say that we moved to Israel from America to upgrade our lifestyle – just as there are some aspects I like less and some aspects I detest. Just like life.

The process of becoming an Israeli has allowed me to demystify Israel, to become part of the uncertain experiment of turning the most abnormal people into a nation among nations. But becoming an Israeli has also given me entry into the opposite and no less uncertain experiment – of testing our spiritual exceptionalism. Zionism, after all, promised to fulfill the contradictory longings of the Jews: To make us a normal nation and a light to the nations. I embrace that paradox as the defining principle of my Israeli identity, perhaps the animating force of Israeliness.

On my aliyah flight, when the plane began its descent, I was struck with a blinding headache. It was a strange moment: I wasn't prone to migraines before or since. When I closed my eyes, it got worse: blinding streaks of pain. After we landed, the pain slowly receded. I've often thought back to that moment. Was it an intimation of the upheavals to come – living through missile attacks and terrorism, becoming a soldier and the father of a soldier – and expressed in the phrase, *Eretz Yisrael niknet b'yisurim*, the land of Israel is won through suffering? Or was it a kind of revelatory moment – a literal flash of light – a promise of what this land can reveal if you work hard enough on yourself to be able to receive?

Becoming an Israeli reinforced my longing for a God-centered life. Shortly after settling into Jerusalem, Sarah and I joined a Jewish meditation circle, and we have been part of that work ever since. True, God's Name is often abused here by politicians and zealots and religious functionaries; yet this is a land that takes religion seriously and can nurture the spiritual aspirant. Unlike most places in the West, here the quest for God doesn't require a constant battle against the prevailing ethos, but aligns you with an essential element of the culture.

The growing spiritual search in Israeli society is increasingly reflected in our popular music. In its formative years, Hebrew music was the carrier of the secular Zionist ethos; today it is the carrier of the rejudaization of Israeli culture. Many of our leading singers and composers – Berry Sakharof, Ehud Banai, Evyatar Banai and the late Meir Banai (anyone named Banai), and Shai Tsabari, Etti Ankri, Shuly Rand and Morin Nehedar – are now writing contemporary prayers. God has become a major protagonist in Israeli song.

Taking ownership of Hebrew music, in all its stages, has become an essential part of my absorption into Israeliness. There is a Hasidic story about a deaf man who peers into a wedding hall and, seeing celebrants prancing about, is convinced they're all mad. I've come to realize that you can't really understand Israel without knowing its soundtrack.

Living in a Jewish-majority state has given me the self-confidence to be generous in my Jewishness, to step out of the closed circle of victimhood in which I, as the son of a Holocaust survivor, was raised. As an Israeli, I've been deeply involved in interfaith work with Muslims and Christians – once inconceivable to me. That work was made possible by Zionist empowerment, by the realization that Jewish sovereignty has, to some extent, reversed our historic relationship with Christianity and Islam, so that we are now the majority, responsible for Christian and Muslim minorities.

The renewal of power has been a hard gift to the Jewish people, depriving us of the purity of victimhood. But that was a false innocence, untested by the temptations of power – precisely as Yehudah Halevi worried in *The Kuzari*. I don't minimize the agonizing moral dilemmas we face. But being an Israeli means taking responsibility – for our failures as well as successes.

I have never regretted my decision to come, never looked back. Not because I forced myself into a rigid ideological mode. If anything, the opposite process has happened – the more I got to know the complexity of Israel and its challenges, the less certain I became. Still, I've felt the pull of home so strongly that America lost its ability to evoke in me even nostalgia.

We "Anglo" immigrants are a tiny proportion of Israeli

society. And yet each voice in this book is a vital expression of faith in the Jewish state. We are Israelis by choice, rather than by birth or force of circumstance. Each of us, simply by leaving the safety and prosperity of our countries of origin, has proven the depth of the Jewish people's love for this land. However few our numbers, we are an indispensable affirmation of the rightness of the Jewish return home.

Making aliyah is a form of making love. Every person in this book first fell in love with the *idea* of a Jewish state. But that is never enough to sustain aliyah; all of us who remain have also fallen in love with the *reality* of a Jewish state. The writers of this book are our great contemporary lovers of Zion.

Why did we come? Because the voice of our beloved was calling, and we live in the time when it is possible to answer.

Packing for Aliyah

Bring Ziplocs

JESSICA LEVINE KUPFERBERG

Jessica, a former litigation attorney, made aliyah from La Jolla, California with her family in July 2014 after a chance encounter in Hawaii brought them an opportunity to fulfill their dream. Jessica is a writer and popular blogger at The Times of Israel and her work has appeared on Kveller.com, Aish.com, *The Jewish Journal of Los Angeles*, *Forward.com*, and J.weekly.

Bring Ziplocs.

And a plethora of patience, a reservoir of resilience, a serious sense of humor. And of course, proper documentation.

Bring your old yearbooks, your favorite face cream, and some good English books.

Bring sturdy backpacks (but *not* the kind with wheels on them) and sharpies and pens, but not other school supplies because they are *very* specific about the kind of pencil case your kid will need and the holes in your old binders and the new papers here are totally different and don't line up.

You'll see that sometimes, things from before just don't line up.

Bring cans of white tuna, a few beloved Trader Joe's treats, sneakers for when your current ones wear out.

And bring your sense of adventure.

Yes, soon you will be busy with the absorption offices, the bank, the utility companies, and your driver's license. You will be frustrated when your lift is late, or your couch was left off your lift, or they won't release the car you imported because only Mahmood can do it, and Mahmood won't be back until next Tuesday.

You will cry. You will miss your people back there.

But you'll singe your lips on piping hot shawarma. You will sniff the rows of spices at a shuk, take free morsels of sweet halva and have to stop yourself from going back for more. You will sting at the Dead Sea, hear the rush of ancient waterfalls, and dance with a bar mitzvah boy winding his way through the maze of the Old City. You will drink upside down coffee in a little cafe in the north, get sunburned in Eilat. Wipe the sweat from your brow at a gleaming port in Tel Aviv and then brush snowflakes from your hair in Jerusalem as you wait for a bus. You will burst when you see the hills erupt in the red *kalaniot* that herald spring. You will pick holy grapes and cherries and pack food for the poor. You will slip on worn cobble stone streets and feel small next to new imposing buildings bearing glossy ads that beckon you to shop, to buy, to switch plans.

You will laugh when you use the wrong word and you will *mamash* cry again when your kids use the right ones in their new language.

You will climb mountains and traverse valleys. And you will see the birds nesting in the old stones of the Kotel, and when you touch the Wall for the first time after your flight here you will whisper to G-d:

I did it. I'm here. I am home.

So bring your grandmother's crystal bowl, your family pictures, a gas barbecue if you dare.

Bring some moxie – no, *chutzpah* – so you get ahead in line, or even get into the right line in the first place.

And bring your faith and your hopes and your dreams.

And don't worry.

Remember that what you are searching for – you'll find it here, somehow. The cost may be greater, but yes, it is worth it.

What you really, truly need, you will get here, at home.

Except for, maybe, the Ziplocs.

Laughing and Crying Through Aliyah

Ariane Mandell

Ariane is a breaking news editor at *The Jerusalem Post*. She holds degrees in East Asian studies and comparative religion, and is an alumna of the Tikvah Institute for Zionist Thought and Leadership at Ein Prat and the Dorot Fellowship in Israel. Originally from New Hampshire, USA, she now lives in Tel Aviv. Ariane made aliyah in 2015.

After spending the last year in Israel as a Dorot Fellow, I knew I wanted to make aliyah. I returned to the states for a month to tie up some loose ends, and this coming Monday I'm jumping on a Nefesh B'Nefesh charter flight to my new home in the Middle East.

"American summer!" I thought. I had envisioned long walks with my father and our yellow lab, Huxley, in the park by our house in New Hampshire, languorous shopping trips with mom, board games with my brother, and endless girls' nights.

But that's not how it happened. I raced around getting all the documents together for my aliyah visa, buying barrels of maple syrup for people back in Israel, triple booking friends for coffee dates, and tossing cocktail dresses and bathing suits and Birkenstocks and Torah commentaries and boxes of mac'n'cheese and cold medicine and knick-knacks into overstuffed suitcases, because even after years in Israel, I still haven't quite accepted that there's nothing I could possibly need that I can't find there.

Meeting with friends was elating and difficult. It's like we were never apart. Conversation flowed freely between tight hugs and laughter, and then I saw in their eyes that it hurts them that it won't ever be like it was before. Our friendship will last, but I won't get vegan food with them every Thursday night anymore. I won't be at their birthday parties. I can't bring the rum and ice cream after a breakup, and I can't be the loudest one cheering at their show. They're so happy for me, that I've found a place I feel I belong, but ending every date with "We'll visit! We'll skype!" doesn't change that our friendship must shift.

Things have been tense with my parents all trip. Sometimes we laugh and joke and pass the wine around, in complete denial. Sometimes we scream at each other about incidental things. ("THIS IS A REMAKE OF KUNG FU HUSTLE ON NET-FLIX RIGHT NOW." "NO, IT'S THE ORIGINAL, STOP IT.") And I know we're not fighting about martial arts movies. We're fighting because I'm not their little girl anymore. Or rather, because I'll always be their little girl, but I'm going someplace far away where they can't hold me or protect me anymore. We didn't want to admit that to each other. We didn't want to face head-on that this great and amazing thing I'm doing is a good-bye at the same time that it's a hello.

Finally, I had the expected emotional breakdown. When I couldn't decide which towels to pack, I ran weeping to the backyard, where my dad was tossing the ball into the lake for Huxley to fetch. "What's wrong now?" he asked good-naturedly. "Worried about packing? You're not going to fit everything. That's okay. We can ship you everything in a trunk."

"No," I said, wiping sticky tears from my face. "I always forget things. I can buy them in Israel. Or come home and get them sometime."

"Then what?" he asked. "Stressed about cleaning your room? You'll never finish. I never expected you to. You can come and visit and chip away at your room every year for the rest of your life. Don't worry about it."

Finally, I said. "You know, I talked to my friend Ro last night."

"Oh yeah?" he said, eyes on Huxley's head bobbing above the lily pads.

"Yeah, my friend from Ein Prat. She made aliyah a few years ago. Alone, like me. I asked her if making aliyah was emotional for her, too. I mean, I'm 100% sure of my decision, but it's still so sad. It's making you and Mom so sad, and it makes me sad to see you sad. It's hard, it's been so hard."

My dad sniffed and blinked, hands in the pockets of his overalls.

"And Ro said she cried all the week before she left, she couldn't stop. And if I didn't cry, she'd be worried about me, because she'd be concerned I was coming to Israel for the wrong reasons and I wouldn't make it. She said people who run away from their lives don't make it in Israel, but I have a life and a family that loves me, it's just that my home is somewhere else, and it's extremely confusing and emotional to leave that behind."

My dad cleared his throat.

"She said it's good that I cried, because my parents need to know I'm going to miss them, that it's comforting for them to know that I'm not running from them and that it's not something they did that made me pull away."

He was quiet for several moments, and then he said, "Okay, first: You told me you would never ever go through another New England winter. You know, we got ten feet of snow last year, and I really can't blame you for leaving. Number two: People say to me stupid shit like, 'Gee, Israel, isn't it dangerous?' And I say, 'Well, I don't know… I mean, Ariane called me after the first bomb at the Boston Marathon went off, saying, "Dad, I'm alright!" and in the background I heard the second bomb going off.' You can get collected any place."

"Collected?"

"It's a figure of speech. Number three: Israel is a very interesting place. I grew up with a host of stereotypes about Jews. And you can never really shake them until you go to Israel. And you meet all these different people, and they speak different languages, and come from different countries, and they're brain surgeons and garbage men and farmers, and they're all Jews. Tel Aviv is a wild city, and Jerusalem is super-mystical, and even if the world's got a problem with Israel, there's all these Israelis around you and you're all in the same boat, whereas when you're in the Diaspora, you face the same enemies, but you're alone. And it's a very different environment."

He watched Huxley race across the yard, digging in the mud, as he continued. "Now, regarding my family's desire to go to Israel… My grandfather liked steel, he was a metalsmith. He decided to make himself a boat, to go to Israel. It was HUGE, you know? I saw it with my own eyes, in the garage. It was supposed to be launched in the Connecticut River, and he was going to sail to Israel. And then his sons gave him a ticket to go to Miami, and he was really happy there, and he said 'Well, it's not Israel, but it is the Garden of Eden here.' I don't know what happened to the boat. It was his dream to go to Israel, but he got distracted. So you're fulfilling that dream."

And he looked right at me when he said, "I'm proud of you, because it's what you want to do! Lots of people sit at home and think, 'Gee I'd like to…' and you do it. I don't usually *like* the things you do, Ariane. I didn't *like*, for example, when you went alone, a Jewish woman, to Jordan last summer. CLEVER MOVE. Do you know what could have happened?!? AN INTERNATIONAL CRISIS!"

"Focus on Israel, Dad."

"I'm proud of you because you're not chickening out. Does anyone have a real desire to do anything? You do. So do it. RALLY!"

Later that night, I gave my mom a big hug in the kitchen, and I said, "I'm sad, too. And I'm sorry."

And it was like the emotional blockade was broken, and she said, "I don't want you to be *sorry*. I feel like … like I'm sending you into the wilderness, you know? And I don't like that, as a mom. It makes me sad, and anxious, and worried. But I don't want you to feel *sorry* that you're going. I'm glad you're doing what you want to do. I'm glad that you feel very strongly about it. I'm glad there are people across the ocean who seem to care about you and look after you. You have some very good friends there, they've looked after you for years now. That makes me feel good, too. And then I'm very sad. I say to myself, you said goodbye to her last time, and she went away for so long … maybe this time will be shorter, because she'll visit soon."

To which my dad added, "HEY, she's definitely going to go SOMEWHERE. FLORIDA. Or SOUTHERN CALIFORNIA. Somewhere it doesn't snow. It may as well be Israel. Look, Ariane, I don't know *anyone* who was here last winter that wants to be here *this* winter."

And I started laughing and crying at the same time.

I didn't want to introduce myself to you this way. I wanted to be the picture of the smiling olah, I wanted you to believe that this isn't hard. Or, maybe, *I* wanted to believe it isn't hard. But it *is* hard. And I'm doing it anyway, because I want to so badly, because I love Israel and I want to be part of it, because it's the right thing to do, because it's my dream and I have the chance to live it. And I'm the kind of girl who takes those chances, like Ro is, like all olim do.

I'm laughing, I'm crying, I'm racing to the airport.

Making Aliyah: Here Goes ... Everything!

Eliana Rudee

At just 19 years old, Eliana founded a five-college pro-Israel club, where her programming for the event "Less Hamas More Hummus" was picked up by CAMERA and is now replicated on countless university campuses across North America. At 21, Eliana spoke at the Israeli Presidential Conference about the future of Jewish leadership. Eliana made aliyah in 2015 and works as a journalist for the Haym Salomon Center, writing about Israel and Jewish issues.

Tomorrow, I make aliyah. The next day, I become an Israeli citizen. And the day after that, I begin my life in Israel.

Nervous? Definitely. Excited? To say the least. Ready? As much as I'll ever be!

It took two whole weeks to pack. I began by piling all my belongings onto my ping-pong table; and when everything I owned was stacked into a pile, I stopped, stood in front of it all, and stared.

This was the sum total of my things in one large mass, everything physical that defines my life. It was difficult to transfer everything into the suitcases, knowing it all would soon be leaving the home in which I grew up – the home in which I took my first steps, learned to read, put on plays with my brother, celebrated holidays, dressed up for high school dances, and the home to which I returned during college breaks.

After finally stuffing everything in, I glanced at my packed-to-the-brim suitcases and wondered if I had packed the right things – I had my clothes, electronics, kitchenware, toiletries, and probably a million Ziploc bags. I had researched and researched (and researched) what to bring with me and even found many checklists of things to bring. I ran through the checklist once more, and yes, I had everything.

I turned toward the mirror to look at the last thing moving to Israel – me. I wondered, "My suitcases are ready. Am *I* ready?" There were no checklists to determine if *I* had the right intangibles necessary to be successful in Israel. Like my luggage, I was also leaving my home and family. But, unlike my suitcases, I am filled with things like experience, education, and fortunately a lot of support from my friends and family. "But will it be enough?" I wondered.

That momentary "Oh my God, what am I doing?" thought shot through me like a shock wave and landed in the pit of my stomach. I shook my head and reminded myself of why I am doing this.

In Israel, more than anywhere else in the world, I am filled with a sense of wonder, community, and purpose. That pure bliss you feel when you learn something amazing, fall in love, or accomplish something of significance is how I often feel in Israel. It's a natural high, and it feels right. Perhaps everyone has a place like that, and I know that for many Jews like myself, that place is Israel. What pulls us there isn't easily explainable, but it's a powerful feeling. And if I *didn't* follow that feeling, that's when I should really be asking myself, "Oh my God, what am I doing?" After all, isn't life about following those gut feelings?

Moving to Israel will be extremely, incredibly challenging, but we learn from challenge. We grow from challenge. And in Israel, there are lots of them: constant chance of war, required army service, high living costs, high taxes, and scarce natural resources. For an immigrant, we can also add to that list acclimating to a new culture, learning a difficult language, navigating a foreign bureaucracy, and living apart from family and friends. So let's hope the extreme challenges do indeed translate into extreme learning!

As I leave for Israel tomorrow, I know that if there is any "thing" I am missing, I can acquire it in Israel. Most important is the self-confidence that I will be able to acclimate and succeed, nurtured by the incredible support networks back home, and reinforced by the people of Israel who will be at the airport to greet me with open arms.

Why I'm Making Aliyah

Alex Ryvchin

Alex was born in Kiev, Ukraine. His family left the Soviet Union as refugees and refuseniks in 1987, when Alex was three years old. He went on to study law and politics at the University of New South Wales. He served as a spokesman for the Zionist Federation UK, founded The Jewish Thinker opinion website and was awarded a prestigious Israel Research Fellowship. His writings have appeared in leading publications in Australia and throughout the world.

What compels one to make aliyah?

Is it a decision of the mind? After all, Israel is at the forefront of academia, medicine, renewable energy, and just about every other field worthy of devotion. It is a land of opportunity.

Or is it a matter of the heart? The land where you realize the Zionist vision, give yourself over to the Jewish ancestral home, and come to raise a family in the center of Jewish life.

All of these considerations drove my decision, for Israel is both a land of infinite possibilities and a place of refuge. But there's also something else: I'm tired of sighing.

You see, in every country where I have lived, my national identity has been at the core of both how I have viewed myself and how society has viewed me.

Time and time again, I would be posed the question, "Where are you from?" And, in response, I would sigh, pause, and then unleash my complex personal narrative, complete with a polemic on the delicate interplay between race, religion, culture, language, and countries of birth and residence.

The sigh has come to represent my struggle to understand my national identity as a Jew living in the Diaspora.

There's only one way I can only explain why I found such torment in this seemingly trivial inquiry:

We live in a world obsessed with questions of race, religion, and national identity. We believe that in order to understand ourselves, what we are destined to become, and why we act the way we do, we must explore our roots, our origins. The answer to where we are going lies in where we have already been.

Equally so, national identity dominates the way that we perceive others. For better or worse, we assume that by knowing where someone comes from, we can draw conclusions about their morals, their values, their tolerance of others, even their dietary practices and countless other characteristics.

In the country of my birth, Ukraine, the trouble of defining one's national identity was conveniently simplified by the state. There, you were the nationality that you were told you were – and there was no escaping that. So, despite possessing an unbroken Ukrainian lineage for as far back as my family could trace, my nationality was always "Jewish." Or "an invalid of the fifth paragraph," as Soviet Jews called themselves – a wry poke at the persecution they faced by virtue of the "nationality" sections of their documents.

By the time my family was taken in by Australia as refugees, though I did not quite know who I was, I certainly knew I was not a Ukrainian.

As a schoolboy in Australia, I found I was relentlessly quizzed as to my origin by bright-eyed classmates perplexed by my curious packed lunches full of smoked meats and the handed down, tassled loafers I wore instead of sneakers. Here,

I would naturally apply the Soviet (or is it Nazi German?) principle that one's nationality is precisely what the authorities deem it to be. I would suggest that I was a "Jew," though with some hesitation, for, even at that age, I had some inkling that to be a Jew meant a complex and mercurial state of existence. But I found that this response, rather than being greeted with hostility, was met with knitted brows, as my inquisitors were less concerned with race than with finding out which distant land I had drifted in from and why on earth I was nibbling smoked mackerel and not peanut butter like everyone else.

So I promptly came to understand that while in the Ukraine I could never be a Ukrainian, in Australia I was warmly accepted as one.

But just as I had grown content in the belief that I was some sort of a Ukrainian, I was forced to reconsider my identity all over again. Innocent childhood curiosity quickly gave way to more sophisticated adolescent inquiries. If I was indeed a Ukrainian as I had claimed, why did my name not end in "ko" and where were the Slavic blue eyes and blond hair?

I could have been happy to answer that I was a Ukrainian of the Jewish variety, but frankly, by this point, I was scarfing down peanut butter like everyone else. I was also in possession of an Australian passport and had begun to resent any implication that I was not an Australian and that my origin should be of any consequence.

And this is a pattern that would be repeated throughout my life in Australia. I never felt like any characterization of my identity was satisfactory. If I said I was "Australian," the next question was always "Yeah, but where are you *really* from?" If I said I was a Jew, I would be told "I wanted to know where you're from – not what your religion is," and if I said I was "Ukrainian," well, I knew better than anyone that that was simply not the case.

"Jewish" is more than a religion.

The next four years of my life would be spent living in London, which did nothing to solve my crisis of identity.

I would still sigh and then diligently explain that I came to London from Australia, the land in which I was raised and that I adored; and yes, I know I don't "look" Australian; that's because I was in fact born in the Ukraine; and yes, I know I don't really look Ukrainian either; that's because I am actually Jewish, descended from a long line of other Jews of Ukrainian and Soviet extraction, and no, "Jewish" is not merely a religion.

As vexing as my battle with the question of identity has been, I don't believe that I am alone in this struggle. Could it really be otherwise given the Jewish condition of exile, statelessness, and absorption into foreign lands for nearly 2,000 years? Could it be otherwise for a people that still has not decided once and for all whether it is a race, a religion, a nation or some hybrid of the three? For a people endowed with an inquisitive nature and a more-than-healthy dose of neurosis?

All of these things leave us questioning the extent to which we can immerse ourselves in the cultures of the countries in which we have come to live without compromising our Jewishness.

Do we assimilate and displace our traditions with those of the host nation, or do we confine ourselves to intellectual ghettos to retain our identity while inevitably attracting fear and hostility from the rest of society in the process? Can we find an appropriate balance between the two?

I don't propose to hold all of these answers. In fact, I have merely evoked that inherent Jewish ability to answer one question with many more. But there is one thing that I do know with perfect clarity: I don't want to sigh any more. And nor will I. I was a Jew first, and I will be a Jew last. And now I will come to live in the Jewish State. I will know what it means to live among my own people. I will apply my energy and my abilities toward strengthening my ancestral home. I will learn to speak the language of my ancient forefathers. I have always been an Israelite but now I will be an Israeli, too.

Catching the Israel Bug

Sarah Sassoon

Sarah is a classic wandering and wondering Jew. She grew up in Sydney, Australia and moved to Johannesburg where she met and married her Prince Charming. Just as she acclimated to Africa, she immigrated yet again, making aliyah in 2015 with her husband and brood of four boys. In between dodging soccer balls, she freelances and blogs about Judaism, her love of Jerusalem and life in Israel. To read more, visit www.sarahsassoon.com.

So, we've made aliyah.

Aliyah is such a loaded word. Literally "aliyah" means to "go up." There's only one country we 'go up' to, and that's *Eretz Yisrael* – the land of Israel. We traverse the world upwards physically in search of something "spiritual." Something that can't be defined. Something that's completely irrational. And we're not alone. In 2014, 26,427 people made aliyah worldwide. Around 180 of them were from South Africa and an equal number were from Australia. Jews from all over the world are emigrating upwards.

How do you make the decision to make aliyah?

People ask if we've been planning our aliyah for a long time. The truth is that it was both a spontaneous, quick decision and yet something we've been planning all our lives. We've caught the Israel bug before, but this time it stayed in our system.

What is the Israel bug? It's quite a dangerous virus, so everyone should be warned. It takes place on an innocent holiday to Israel and manifests as a deep gut feeling that takes over one's heart and mind and urges you to miss the return EL AL flight to your home country. This viral incursion is only cured if you catch your plane and return home. After a few weeks, it eventually dissipates into a vague memory of "it would have been nice" as you relax into your beloved, familiar comfort zone.

We've been bitten by the Israel bug a few times, to the extent that we've investigated possible cities that we'd like to live in (Zichron Ya'akov, Jerusalem), we've interviewed schools, reviewed houses. We've explored going but we never made that final decision, until now.

What's changed? We're older, which doesn't mean that we're wiser, but it does mean that our children are older. We knew that ideally we didn't want to move teenage children. Last year, my husband visited Israel and came back saying, "It's doable. We should go have a look, we should move to Jerusalem." I asked him what he was smoking. I had finally settled down in Johannesburg after thirteen years. To move again and leave everything I'd built felt devastating. "Let's go for our summer holidays," he said. So we went, and we were smitten with the Israel bug once again. We realized that our eldest was eleven, so it was now or never (or at least until our youngest child finished high school).

I realized if we didn't give it a go, I'd regret it for the rest of my life. How many opportunities have I missed because of pussyfooting through life and going with the flow, rather than following my heart and dreams? Of course aliyah is a utopian dream, which often pans out very differently in reality.

Having emigrated once before, I knew it wouldn't be simple. We came back to Johannesburg in January, to our flourishing, mint green garden which is bigger than most Jerusalem parks. And we mourned what we were leaving behind. "We live like kings," I announced to any Joburger who would listen. "Do you realize that we live like kings?" I couldn't stop repeating this, as I thought of the cramped Jerusalem apartments, the symphony of Jerusalem streets which is a beeping, honking cacophony of assertive (read: frustrated, sleep deprived) drivers. The children who run wild in the corridors of Israeli schools, the dog poop that is never picked up until you step in it. The shopkeeper's cries in very fast Hebrew at the shuk that makes it impossible to understand, so you buy whatever he gives you, even if you don't need half a kilo of Indian tea.

Who said moving is easy? A new, very different culture. A new language. A new side of the road to drive on. As my Australian friend who lives in Jerusalem told me, "You have to remember that this is the Middle East."

Yet, I've always felt that Israel is my home. Whether we consciously know it or not, we, as Jews, all have a relationship with Israel. Israel is in my blood. Literally. I'm not the first one in my family to make aliyah. Both sets of my grandparents made aliyah from Baghdad, with Operation Ezra and Nehemiah in 1951. My father lived in Israel from the age of three, my mother was born there. They landed in harsh, post-war conditions, and twenty years later, my father, with the rest of his family, moved to the other "promised land": Sydney, Australia. There, they built their lives in the fair dinkum land of man-size beer; where nobody hooted on the roads and baklava was as foreign as a beep bopping Louis Botha taxi. They learned English, how to eat scones with jam and cream, and the joys of frothy flat white coffee. They chose to be diaspora Jews again and brought with them their Judeo-Arabic songs and prayers 2,500 years old. They cried for the rivers of Babylon that they had to leave, they cried for the shores of Israel that they left, but mainly, in true Australian style, they got on with it.

I was born in Australia, after my father wedded my Israeli mother in Tel Aviv and brought her back to Sydney. I was the second of six children. Looking back, I wonder why my parents didn't speak to me in Hebrew, let alone Arabic. I realize now that they were immigrants, and in those days, especially in white Australia, they didn't want to be different. It's the typical diaspora story. It's the story of survival, of establishing a new identity, and of thriving in the newly adopted country of gold.

In many ways, I grew up very Australian: piping hot fish and chips wrapped in newspaper at Bondi Beach, a hearty addiction to Cadbury chocolate, smoking barbecues at Centennial Park. Yet, in other ways, as the child of Jewish immigrants, I grew up in an alternate world. I went to a Chabad school where there were only two girls with Australian-born parents. The rest of us were first generation Australians, with our parents hailing from all over the world: America, Israel, Russia. My generation were the promising new, who didn't struggle with English. We had a bright future ahead of us on the safe, sparkling shores of the melting pot of multicultural Australia.

But there was the other side. When you pray in Hebrew every day of returning to Zion, of Jerusalem being reestablished, and of the ingathering of the exiles, being Down Under, a good twenty-four hour flight from the Promised Land, makes you feel very, very far away. Far from the Jewish dream, from the world, from any sort of Jewish destiny.

We made that jet lagged, never-ending trip to Tel Aviv almost every year. Via Bangkok and Rome or Greece. When we landed in Israel as children, we were gobsmacked by the ready availability of kosher fast food (which is all that matters when you're a kid), the shops remaining closed on Shabbat just like they were closed in Sydney on a Sunday. The amount of Jews we were surrounded by. The Jewish soldiers who were ours, and we didn't have to be told to "be careful of them."

My young eyes couldn't ignore the obvious difference between Sydney and Kiryat Ono, which is where my mother's family lived. Everyone lived in apartments, to have a house was for Savion, an expensive suburb that my aunt loved driving through in a taxi (of course she didn't own the ultimate luxury of a car in those days). There was one cafe in the area, Kapulski's, that she used to love going to. There was a *makolet* in a rusty, sardine gray tin shed, where an old blind man would sell us sweets, relying on the honesty of us children as we placed our carefully counted coins in his hardened, wrinkled hands. Israel in the eighties was a far cry from the trendy, cutting edge technology hub and coffee culture it's become today.

One of my most surreal childhood memories was a July day when there was a *hamsin*, an extraordinarily hot heat wave, when we lived on cordial ice lollies that we made in glass cups. There was water rationing. All the water was turned off, and a water truck drove down the main road to distribute water. I went with my aunt feeling like Alice in Wonderland with our clanging pots and pans to fill them with the precious, transparent liquid. It felt festive and important to be there. To learn not to waste. Water could run out. I loved those days of waking up with the rooster crowing from the unpaved back streets of Kiryat Ono.

On a plane trip back from Tel Aviv home, I remember discussing with my brothers what rating Israel would get as a country. We decided it wasn't a first world country, nor was it a third world country (after all, how could the country of kosher Bazooka chewing gum be third world?). We concluded that it was a second world country. In many ways, it's still a second world country, with many people living below the poverty line.

Who would go live in a second world country? The call to Israel defies explanation. Having emigrated once, I understand that one can't take emigration lightly. To move countries is to lose your whole identity. Nobody knows who you are. It's almost like dying and being reborn. The key to a successful emigration is what you choose to focus on – the dying and all you've left behind, or the rebirth with its new opportunities.

Emigration is up there with all the great stressful traumas that we face in human life. But I've learnt a lot from having done it once before. It helps to come from a migrant family. It helps to have the legacy of being a wandering Jew.

So here's what I've uncovered about emigration. When you move to a new place, it's a new chance to start again. You can be whoever you want to be, and hopefully it's your best self. However, you can't run away from any issues or problems. Be they financial, emotional, or just those irritating people who drive you crazy. It will all manifest in your new abode. My husband reminds me of this continually. He says, "You don't leave a place, you need to go to a place." You need to want to be there. To invest yourself in the environs, invite people you'd like to meet over for meals and for impromptu coffees, rather than passively waiting for people to welcome you into their busy lives. You create the space that you live in. You create who you are. You create the life you lead.

Of course, I've discovered all this the hard way from my first emigration. That there's no space for victimhood or complaining. You make your choices and live in the present of what you've chosen, because no amount of whinging or whining is going to make things better. I've learned that you must create your home in your heart, so that wherever you are, you are at home. And as I think about this, I realize that I've learned this from my grandmother, Nana Aziza, who left Israel with a heavy chest, always wanting to return. She spent the last healthy years of her life traveling between her children in Sydney and Los Angeles, and her family in Israel. She took her home with her wherever she went, and she finally rested where her heart truly was, which is in Jerusalem today.

When I say, "We are making aliyah," I realize that I'm talking about more than my family's future. I am holding the prayers, hopes, and dreams of many generations. That is my diaspora luggage that I carry with me; our songs of "Next Year in Jerusalem," of traveling in the desert for forty years in order to see the Promised Land. Leaving Johannesburg after thirteen years means saying goodbye to a part of my life which was a special time. A vibrant, close Jewish community, loving family and friends. As I pack my home up, I find myself realizing that my life isn't in my accumulated stuff, it's in the relationships that I carry in my heart. So I take Sydney and Johannesburg with me to Jerusalem, following in the sandy footsteps of my forefathers and mothers. And when I'm overwhelmed, I remember what our good friend, Johnnie Walker, said "A journey of a thousand miles begins with a single step."

The Aliyah Experience:
A Mountain Climber's Dream

Ariella Bracha Waldinger

Ariella left her 26-year career in sales, marketing, and management in 2003, in order to return home to reside in the Jewish homeland with her husband. She left her precious children, twin sister, and grandchildren because she understood that "Life is truly a journey of the soul" and her soul was calling her home. She teaches marriages classes, life skills classes, and hosts monthly Rosh Chodesh gatherings for women. She publishes a blog at comingintothelightofaliyah.wordpress .com where she shares aliyah tips, information, stories of inspiration, and Torah teachings.

Mountain climbing has been touted as one of the finest and most exhilarating opportunities available for climbing enthusiasts, who aspire to see the world from its highest vantage point.

Mountain climbing is marketed in particular to "lovers of high places," as the difficult ascent up the mountain is not for the faint of heart nor the weak of spirit. Mountain climbing is all about the persistence it takes to put hands and feet onto one obstacle after another, to eventually reach the summit of a breathtaking mountain-top panorama. It involves risk, commitment, hardship and extraordinary persistence, while at the same time providing countless uplifting, exhilarating, and, some say, life-altering experiences along the way. The entire process of ascending up the high mountain can ultimately foster a deep, profound sense of self-actualization and renewed self-confidence. Climbing enthusiasts speak of the journey up the mountain as a holy mission, providing great spiritual rewards in its purposeful pursuit.

I didn't realize when I chose to make aliyah that I was signing up for one of the greatest expeditions of my life. No one told me I would be capable of unlocking and activating mental, spiritual, and emotional strengths I never dreamed I possessed, in order to cope with the aliyah challenges of an upward climb.

Choosing to make aliyah is a powerful metaphor for signing up for a mountain climbing expedition. Aliyah is a Hebrew word which means ascent or climb. Aliyah is about raising oneself up to a higher spiritual level in order to meet the heightened holiness embedded in the Holy Land. The Zohar teaches that Eretz Yisrael is the only place where Jews can achieve perfection, for there is chemistry between the nation and the Land. Our Sages state that Eretz Yisrael represents and enables the highest fulfillment of earthly life, whereby the physical is brought into perfect harmony with the soul.

Reaching this level of fulfillment can come about only through the efforts expended in doing the work of refining our character. This holy and worthy endeavor leads to the ultimate peak acquisition of spiritual refinement and self-actualization. This refinement is achieved through hard work and is comparable to the actual process of climbing up a mountain.

The mountain consists of many of the situations and experiences that challenge us along the way as we attempt to settle into a new life in a new country with many unknowns gnawing at our vulnerabilities. The process of tackling the raw materials of our life and confronting our issues is the path that must be taken to reach the summit of self-mastery and happiness. It requires commitment, persistence, patience, and a lofty vision. It is truly a holy mission of epic dimensions, as it is part and parcel of the Divine commandments we accepted at the revelation on Har Sinai when we received the Torah.

The new immigrant, like the mountain climber, must have a clear vision of how to move forward to assure his continued upward mobility. The success of the mission will depend on the sheer force of personal desire to move beyond the challenges that stand in opposition to the climb. But the great comfort to be found in the challenges is that, along the way, your spirit will be awakened by brilliant flashes of inspiration, even as they are looming before your eyes. Stirrings of inner awakening from years of slumber will propel you forward, and, without realizing it, you will emerge into the light of the Holy Land and be drawn into its spiritual vortex. Scaling the mountain of personal challenges gives you access to the self-mastery needed to rise to new levels of self-awareness and Divine consciousness. This affords you the ability to savor the spiritual bounty present in the Holy Land.

Dovid Rosoff, in his book, *Land of Our Heritage*, states that, "As Jews, we must understand that embedded within our DNA is the inner desire to return to our ancestral homeland. It is a spiritual blueprint that resides within us." Our souls are like the bird migrating to its natural habitat, following its inborn instincts, who knows that nothing will prevent it from returning home to reach its ultimate Divine destination.

Aliyah manifests the true path that can lead to spiritual greatness because it forces you, in the process of ascending, to see what you are made of. The pettiness and facades fall away as you catch a glimpse of the core greatness that becomes manifest in the journey up the mountain of challenges. As the process of ascent up the mountain is tackled and surmounted, you can absolutely perceive the world from a higher vantage point. Like the mountain climber who has overcome great obstacles to finally stand atop the highest, most breathtaking panoramic vista, you'll be able to attest to the ultimate satisfaction of achieving your lofty goal. Reaching a deeper understanding through overcoming challenges creates breathless moments of exhilaration. It ultimately allows you to stand atop the summit of G-d's mountain, blanketed in ancestral memory, and to embrace it with all your being. The end result will unearth a newfound humility which lends itself to greater spiritual inspiration and gratitude, as we learn from our Sages that one can only claim his inheritance of Eretz Yisrael when he has been humbled.

Rabbi Menachem Mendel of Vitebsk wrote to his followers, stating that anyone who comes to reside in the Holy Land will be challenged on many levels because the Holy Land is rich in spirituality and holiness. He wrote: "Be aware that many transformations and developments will occur within every person who comes to reside in the Holy Land." He cautions his followers to strengthen their faith and refine themselves to the degree that they truly love the Land of Israel. He says that one must become spiritually worthy of the Land. This is the reason why one must truly be a LOVER OF HIGH PLACES in order to have a successful aliyah. The persistence is aptly rewarded by a pristine vision of a better life in our nation with G-d in the center. The experience is exhilarating, as the pure air of a higher spiritual altitude makes one joyous and wise.

The perils in making aliyah and climbing up the mountain of challenges are nothing compared to the spiritual dangers of not making aliyah. Eretz Yisrael is the only place where you can dwell in the shadow of Hashem and be secure in the covering of the shelter of His wings. NO place on earth can compare with the virtues of Eretz Yisrael, nor its safety. The distinctive atmosphere of the Holy Land allows us to shed the influences of life lived outside the land. From this newly formed, higher, more receptive vantage point, we can receive the strong signals of Divine Providence and guidance present in the Land and experience a more genuine Jewish life.

I believe making aliyah is the greatest, most courageous act of faith and trust a Jew can undertake today. The choice forces us to assess our core values and reason for living. It enables and empowers us to live on the level of our Jewish destiny with every endeavor. It affords us the opportunity to contribute our own unique, individual gifts like a free-will offering on the holy altar. Living in our national homeland brings honor to G-d's name and brings our light into the world. We must strive for true allegiance to our divine, national mission and pledge our full, personal commitment. Fulfilling the Divine will is like climbing a difficult mountain, and it is a strenuous climb, indeed, but it is within our ability, We can do it, if we are willing to make the supreme effort of returning home to our G-d-given land.

ASPIRE TO REACH THE SUMMIT OF LIFE AS A JEW IN THE LAND, AND YOU, TOO, WILL BECOME A LOVER OF HIGH PLACES.

Making Aliyah the Right Way

Elie Klein

> Elie is a proud Zionist, devoted family man, and seasoned
> non-profit public relations specialist living in Beit Shemesh.
> Prior to "the big move," he served as the North American
> Director of the Jewish Agency for Israel's Na'ale/Elite Acad-
> emy program. Elie made aliyah in 2004.

On Election Day, we hosted some friends from the "Old Country" for a classic Israeli barbecue (i.e. the kebabs were plentiful
but there wasn't a single hamburger bun in sight). The weary
travelers were at the tail end of a week-long pilot trip (a largely
successful fact-finding mission that will hopefully set the stage
for a smooth and uneventful absorption process this coming
summer) and their heads were absolutely spinning. They were
exhausted and we only had a few hours to spend together before
they had to jet (literally), so we got right down to business.

While the rest of the country was swept up in the excitement of the early exit poll results, we feasted on Freedom Fries,
downed Democracy Dogs, and dissected aliyah from every
angle. (We also binged on Bureaucracy Burgers.)

We covered the usual ground at first – housing costs, job
market, schooling options, lift size, furniture and appliances to
purchase before the move – but took a very interesting detour
when we began discussing living in an "Anglo Bubble" and
raising bilingual kids.

At a lavish restaurant meal with some relatives a few days earlier (it seems that "Pilot Trip" is Latin for "You pick up the tab"), our friends were told that their absorption would be a dismal failure if they decided to settle in an Anglo neighborhood. The logic being that their children would be utterly confused by the "culture clash" and would experience great difficulty acclimating and developing normally. And, if their children were to somehow defy the odds and persevere, they would identify as Israelis and would be unable to relate to or communicate with their American parents.

Our friends, who had already set their sights on an Anglo haven in Efrat, seemed genuinely concerned by the possibility that this analysis was even partially based in reality.

Upon hearing this, I asked if these relatives had settled in an all-Israeli neighborhood themselves, and if they struggled for years to make it work. Though I was pretty confident that both questions would be answered in the affirmative, I smiled when my suspicions were confirmed.

It was at this point that I shared the following insight with them.

Over the last four and a half years, I have observed that olim (myself included) constantly redefine success in the aliyah process (a continuum of challenges that only really ends with a much more substantial move "Upstairs") in relation to what they themselves are doing and have accomplished. In fact, even those who whine and complain throughout the process will more than likely try to convince others later on that the steps they took are crucial to making aliyah "the right way."

The reason, of course, is that the daily battles we wage as olim (everything from a conversation with a cell phone company, to surviving parent-teacher conferences, to finding a job) are hard fought and seldom won. In order to calm and reassure ourselves, we strongly encourage others to follow our lead as though we have unlocked the secrets of the universe.

But the notion that there can be one perfect way to approach any element of the aliyah experience is truly ludicrous. There are simply too many variables that factor into how the absorption process unfolds – including the ages of those immigrating, level of their proficiency in Hebrew, liquidity of their funds, job market demand for their chosen professions, strength of their support system, stability of the housing market, availability of educational and medical resources in their part of the country, and the composition and agenda of the sitting government (to name just a few) – for there to be a one-size-fits-all solution for the hurdles encountered.

Indeed, aliyah experiences are like snowflakes – they appear similar, even identical, from a distance. But, under the microscope, it becomes clear that they are intricate and entirely unique. No two absorptions will ever be the same. (Children are also like snowflakes, but that's for another post.)

It is for this reason that I encouraged our pilot-tripping pals to focus on only one aliyah experience – their own. I acknowledged that asking for advice from those who have "been there" is, of course, key to success in any process, but suggested that the advice received from fellow olim should be run through an industrial-grade sifter.

And now, dear reader, I encourage you to do the same.

If you are "putting in your *hishtadlut*," making every effort to acclimate to your new life thousands of miles away from everything you once knew so well, then you are headed in the right direction.

If you are making informed decisions and are left feeling

generally satisfied by their outcomes, then you are no doubt on the correct path.

And if you wake up every morning ready to face the inevitable gauntlet of uniquely Israeli challenges that await you throughout your day (rather than cowering in fear or curling up into the fetal position and wishing it all away), then you have made it on your own terms.

The aliyah trail that you blaze with your blood, sweat, and tears *is* "the right way" ... for you. And don't let any outspoken, advice-slinging oleh tell you differently.

Not even me.

Aliyah to a Courtyard

Shayna Driscoll

Shayna is originally from Brooklyn, New York. After participating in a Birthright trip in 2010, she was inspired to one
day live in Israel. She graduated Binghamton University in
2012, where she received a degree in Political Science. She
attended the Mayanot Women's Program in Jerusalem, after
which she returned to New York to work as a fundraiser for
UJA-Federation of New York, where she spent three years
overseeing philanthropic campaigns at two major Wall Street
firms. Shayna made aliyah in the summer of 2016.

I turned 25 in November and did what any rational twen-
ty-something does on their birthday: I stood on a chair at my
synagogue, at a Shabbat *Kiddush* in my honor, hugging a bottle
of Jack Daniel's, and gave a monologue. I know how this sounds,
but I have always had a flare for the dramatic and now know it
was most likely the peak of a quarter-life crisis. I handed out
l'chaims (aka shots taken in the name of life) and proclaimed
boldly to my friends and neighbors that in this new year, I would
start doing things that scared me.

I explained how a recent first-time camping trip changed
my perception of my comfort zone. I was the girl who walked
through life proclaiming herself a JAP but, in reality, actually
loves the outdoors and lying in the grass for hours. I don't
necessarily need a shower and proper septic system to be my

happiest self. I'll admit, I slept in three layers and tied a hoodie up to my nose for fear of spiders, but at least I was trying!

What had stopped me from experiencing it all before? Literally, myself and, perhaps, seasonal allergies. It wasn't until I stood on that chair and was accountable to my community that I realized I wasn't pushing myself hard enough. I was racing through life on auto-pilot, from one goal and achievement to another, without really experiencing the moments that make life so exciting. That's because the moments that constitute change can also be the scariest. Who would actively choose to be scared if they didn't have to be? That's just nuts.

I challenged my friends and neighbors to be vulnerable. I told them to start doing things far out of their comfort zone, to escape their self-defined "box." All that sounds easy until it became a real promise to myself, not just a speech.

True to my words, I started immediately after Shabbat. I went after something I really wanted that was way out of my realm of comfort, but which also scared me enough to make me want to puke. Excellent criteria.

I asked a guy out. Well, it was more like I demanded he go out with me, but whatever, I am a generally aggressive person and was on a vulnerability high. You know what? It felt really darn good, minus the getting rejected part.

In the weeks leading up to all this, Israel saw an influx of stabbings and car rammings. One of those Friday nights, I skipped my Shabbat meal and instead spent the night at my favorite place in Brooklyn. A place where nobody can see or hear me, but where I feel my voice is strongest.

I stood on the roof of my apartment and screamed at G-d. My tears weren't just for my brothers and sisters in Israel but also for myself. I begged to know – what on earth was I doing in New York? What was stopping me from being in Israel? I felt desperate, like I was slowly suffocating.

The emotions soon subsided, and I returned to my auto-pilot state. I told myself that staffing an upcoming Birthright trip would fix how I felt. Meanwhile, my perfect plan was enacted. I would spend the next few years at my amazing job while getting my master's degree in public service at my dream school, get married, build my savings, and one day move to Israel.

That logical plan quickly fell apart the moment I stepped off the plane and saw myself kissing the ground.

The frequency of stabbings in Jerusalem prevented us from praying at the Western Wall for Friday night services, a Birthright signature moment. As a *madricha* (counselor) it pained me that the participants couldn't experience this. In an effort to basically make shawarma out of vegetables, we took them to a synagogue courtyard in Nachlaot, Jerusalem to sing at the top of our lungs.

It was beautiful but sad. I knew what could be going on outside that courtyard but tried to forget it, to be present. It was unexpected and different, but it was incredibly real and raw.

In the morning, I returned to the courtyard to pray at its shul. As I left services, I paused to make a mental photograph of the dozens of families in the courtyard below. Smiling women in their flowing head scarves watching their husbands chase after their babies.

Outside that courtyard, a fellow Jew could be getting attacked in her own home, in front of her young children, or a fearful man could be walking with his *yarmulka* hidden in his pocket. But that moment in the courtyard was their present and they were making it count, with both grace and pride.

As I watched, it hit me. What I was witnessing was a life of difficulty but also one of meaningful easiness. I knew what I had to do, and it wasn't part of my plan. It wouldn't be solely for my love of the State of Israel or to help unite the Jewish people. Do I believe that, as a Jewish woman, I have the unique privilege of creating a life for my future generations in the Land we finally got back after thousands of years? Yeah, definitely!

But, if I am being honest, the real reason I am leaving so much behind – family, a promising career, a prestigious degree and inspirational friends – is for the chance at life in the courtyard. A challenging life, full of passion and chance, commitment and resolve, fear and achievement, tears and laughter.

Ironically, as I sat in a cab leaving the Jewish Agency with my aliyah approval in hand, I received a congratulatory acceptance email from my dream graduate school. I could literally see two diverging roads in my path and was able to imagine my life at the end of each.

I was being given a real choice, and both answers would be the right one. I believe deeply in *Hashgacha Pratit* (Divine Providence), so, in my mind, the outcome of my life would always be the same, and I would still end up in Israel. But what would the journey there be like? With that in mind, in the language of my fellow millennials, I swiped right for Israel.

If there is one thing I learned upon making this decision, it is that if you can't go a day without thinking about something, no matter how scary it is, it's a pretty clear sign you should do something about it. Life will happen no matter what, and you only get one chance to be part of it.

So, when you are 120 years old, I sure hope that you look back from your own courtyard and say you would do it all again, but maybe minus the bottle of Jack. *L'chaim*.

Aliyah to Everest

Alan Rosenbaum

> Rabbi Alan Rosenbaum is the vice-president of Davka Corpo-
> ration (www.davka.com) one of the world's leading developers
> of Jewish educational software. He has lived in Israel since
> 1996, and writes extensively about Jewish life in Israel for *The
> Jerusalem Post*, The Times of Israel, and other publications.

Towering 29,029 feet above sea level, Mount Everest has been
dubbed "the roof of the world." Over the past few years, I have
read a number of books about the challenges and dangers of
climbing Everest – so much so that I have become hooked
on the subject. I have even expressed my interest in someday
reaching the summit. These remarks have usually been met with
amused stares and snickering from family members. Clearly,
they think, I have lost my marbles. Climbing Mount Everest is a
wild fantasy for an acrophobic, balding 56-year-old male, who is
not particularly sure-footed and doesn't do well in cold weather.
Yet, despite the unlikelihood of ever seeing Mount Everest, let
alone scaling its heights, I persist in my irrational belief that I
will someday make it to the top.

Twenty years ago this July, after reading a number of books
on the subject, my wife and I, together with our children,
embarked on what seemed to be an equally unlikely quest –
moving to Israel. Leaving behind family, friends, and business
interests, we packed our belongings and made the switch from
the Middle West to the Middle East. Clearly, some of our friends

thought, this was a wild fantasy for a balding, 36-year-old male who was not particularly aggressive, and insisted on speaking with a flat *reish* pronunciation. Yet, despite the seeming irrationality of that decision, here we still are, 20 years later.

Why do people want to climb Mount Everest? Why do people want to move to Israel? When it comes to Everest, George Mallory, the famous British climber, is reputed to have answered, "Because it's there." The simple fact that Everest exists is reason enough for people to want to meet the challenge. When it comes to Israel, people provide a variety of different answers.

Some people will say that they moved to Israel for religious reasons. God promised it to Abraham and his descendants, they state, and we are fulfilling that promise. Others may say that they came for nationalistic reasons. Israel was the home of the Jewish people for thousands of years, and now that it has been renewed, we should be here. Still others have come because they are running away from something in their land of origin – be it from family or from a difficult personal situation. Regardless, while climbing Everest and moving to Israel do not present the same level of danger, I think that moving to Israel represents the ultimate *Jewish* challenge.

Recently, Mount Everest has gotten some bad press. In 2015, there were no ascents, due to a series of avalanches, and in May of this year, several fatalities were reported there. Moreover, an article appeared in *The New York Times*, which indicated that by at least one measurement, the world's highest peak is not Everest, but rather Mount Chimborazo, in Ecuador. Despite these difficulties, climbing Everest remains the ultimate goal of high altitude mountain climbers.

And, like Everest, life in Israel is not perfect. Corruption and dishonesty in government are rife. Religious matters are often complicated. The threat of terrorism is always present, many of the neighboring countries would prefer to see us vanish, and local customer service representatives – if such a thing exists – usually do not wish callers 'a nice day' when the call is concluded. Yet, despite the difficulties involved and the sometimes tarnished appearance that Israel may sometimes present, moving to Israel is the Everest of Jewish challenges. Why? Because, ultimately, just like Everest, it's there. Historically, religiously, culturally, geographically – Israel represents the center of Judaism and the Jewish people. And for some, that is a challenge that they can't resist.

Moving to Israel, like climbing Mount Everest, is not for everyone. But just as Everest represents a goal and an achievement – even for those who, like me, may never make it to the top – Israel should, ideally, represent a goal and an objective, even for those who may never move there.

If you're reading this, and you can't, or don't want to, live in Israel for whatever reason, you can still follow Israel from afar. Read about Israel in the news, visit Israel if you can, speak about Israel, argue about Israel, get hooked on Israel. Like climbing Everest, living in Israel may not be for everyone. But, like Everest, it's "there," and we can all appreciate it, regardless of where we live.

As for me? After 20 years, while I have a bit more "chutzpah" than I had when we first arrived, my children still laugh at my *reish*. Some things, I guess, never change.

Settling In

A Day in the Life of an Oleh

Akiva Gersh

I love making aliyah.

I say "making" and not "made" because I believe that aliyah is not a static one-time event that begins and ends when our plane lands at Ben Gurion Airport and, for the first time, we don't have a return ticket home.

Aliyah is a process. An exciting and inspiring process but also a humbling process that finds many of us olim taking a few life-steps back in order to learn how to live and survive in this new environment. One that on the soul/emotional level is so familiar to us, is so much our deepest home, but on the everyday gotta-get-stuff-done-and-live-here level is so different from the worlds we left behind. Aliyah is a process of learning all over again, of acclimating and acculturating, of celebrating our large and small accomplishments and feeling frustrated when it seems like nothing's working. Of forgetting at times why we even made aliyah... and then remembering exactly why we made aliyah and knowing that any and all sacrifices and challenges we experience along the way are more than worth it.

With that in mind, I take you through a typical day of my life here in Israel. As an oleh. Because as olim, we see things that native Israelis don't. We notice those moments that others either take for granted or aren't even aware of. We *kvell* over Jews openly being Jews in the Jewish state. We smirk at the humorous mannerisms of sabras. And we get emotional witnessing our children growing up in this land.

So, here's a day in the life of this oleh:

6:00 – Wake up. From the bathroom window, hear the sounds of construction workers getting ready for another day. How early are they legally allowed to begin?

6:15 – On the way to the train, pass those same construction workers making coffee over a little fire they made from scrap wood from their work site. They offer me some of their piping hot coffee served in a thin crinkled plastic cup. I politely decline.

6:35 – Wait at the train station for the train to Tel Aviv. Wonder why no one is really dressed like they're going to work. (Is it possible that everyone here works for start-ups?)

6:40 – On the train. Pass a woman wearing pants and a tank top reciting Psalms. Sitting behind her is a girl wearing a long skirt with her face buried in her siddur, rocking back and forth. Across from her an Arab woman wearing a hijab is reading her free copy of *Yisrael HaYom*. (I think to myself that my Hebrew will probably never be as good as hers.)

6:42 – Take out my tallit and tefillin to start my own morning prayers. Of course, no one stares. In fact, the guy sitting across from me asks if he can put on my tefillin when I'm done.

6:55 – Look around the train. All kinds of wires are dangling from the train's outlets. 97% of the passengers are looking either at a smartphone, a laptop, or a Kindle. Some are simultaneously using two of the three. The dings of WhatsApp messages ring through the air. The Start-Up Nation is already beginning another day of work.

7:30 – On my second train to Hod HaSharon. Someone is watching a YouTube video at full volume without headphones. I wait for someone to say something to him, but no one does. Does this not bother anybody else?? I wait longer. Surely someone, in his or her beautiful native Hebrew, will say something to him. But no one does. So I, the person on the train with the least developed Hebrew, get up from my seat and ask him to put on headphones. Miraculously, he does. He saves me from having to argue with him in Hebrew.

7:40 – A guy sits next to me with sunglasses, ripped jeans and lots of piercings. He has "*Shema Yisrael*" tattooed in Hebrew on his arm.

8:00 – Get off the train in Hod HaSharon and start my 15-minute walk to work. Pass the owner of the one store in town that sells pork opening up his shop. Before entering, he kisses the mezuzah.

8:05 – Phone rings. Person is speaking Russian. Wrong number.

8:06 – Phone rings again. Person is speaking Arabic. Wrong number.

8:07 – Phone dings (dings, not rings). Text message from my 10-year-old son just saying hi on the way to school. In Hebrew. I smile.

8:10 – Stop at the bakery to pick up a little something. A friend of mine who made aliyah just a few weeks ago calls as I'm paying so I don't pick up. A minute later, my phone dings announcing the message he just left on my voicemail. I smile. He'll soon learn that no one in Israel leaves or listens to voice messages.

8:20 – Arrive to work. The guard at the gate has a newspaper and a copy of the Zohar on his table. Next to a pack of cigarettes.

8:25 – Talk with a few of my Israeli colleagues in the office. One starts telling a joke in Hebrew. I get a little nervous, but I'm ready. He gets to the punchline and… I understand the joke! I laugh more in celebration of understanding than at the actual joke itself.

8:30 – Start my day at the Alexander Muss High School in Israel, where I teach students from America about Jewish history and modern Israel. Before my first lesson with a new group officially begins, I introduce them to the song, *"Kvish HaHof"* (a popular Israeli hip-hop song). And then we talk about why Avraham was given the mission of starting an entirely new religion. I love my job.

16:30 – Start my long journey home after a visit to the archaeological site, Tel Gezer, where I show my students 3000-year-old pieces of pottery made by the ancient Israelites (I love my job).

17:15 – Wait in In Tel Aviv for my train home. After a 15-minute delay, and a large crowd of impatient commuters forms, the train arrives. Doors open up and it is packed to the brim with people. The people on the train are standing like falafel balls stuffed tightly into a pita. They stare at us staring back at them from the platform. We all want to get on. "There's absolutely no room," one woman says with a hint of pride in her voice. I and another person push our way on anyway.

17:18 – Feeling good about my strategic use of Israeli *chutzpah*. Sure, someone's backpack is pressing deeply into my chest, making breathing very difficult, but at least I'll get home faster.

17:21 – Three minutes later, the train comes to a complete stop. The conductor announces that there are electrical issues with the train and it could be a while before it's fixed. Great, with half the train standing, this could be a total disaster. But it's not. Instead, everyone around me starts making jokes and everyone, who just minutes ago were total strangers to each other, begins laughing and having a grand ol' time. It's really unbelievable. *Am Yisrael Chai.*

17:48 – After 30 minutes of having a grand ol' time, one guy can't take it anymore and screams out, "I'm getting out of here!" He pushes his way through the crowd and presses the emergency button, which sends the train's doors flying open. He jumps off. The whole train goes silent in shock. He makes his way to the side of the tracks and starts walking.

17:50 – Two minutes later, the train starts moving again.

17:52 – We pass the man walking along the tracks. Everyone waves to him. He doesn't wave back.

18:25- Finally get off at my stop. I stand outside the station and engage in the Israeli pastime of *tremping* (hitchhiking). Eventually a sweet older Sephardi guy stops and gives me a ride. Noticing my American accent, he begins to tell me how he was born in a tent that his family lived in for the first few years after they came to Israel from Tunisia. This was before the country could afford to give them more permanent housing. He concludes his brief autobiography by telling me that his grandson graduated the Technion (Israel's version of MIT) and is now working for a leading hi-tech company. His story is the story of Israel.

18:45 – Finally arrive home and sit down for a family dinner. Listen to my kids share about their day. Realize that almost every sentence out of their mouths is a masterful blend of Hebrew and English, to the point that English-only or Hebrew-only speakers would have no idea what they're saying.

19:30 – My son's friend calls. Asks if he can come over now for a play date. At 7:30 in the evening?? Really?? I tell him, "No."

20:00 – My daughter has some questions about her homework before she goes to bed. I sit down next to her, open up Google Translate on my phone, and get to work.

22:00 – Realize I need to ask my son's teacher a question. Wonder if it's too late to text her. A bit nervously, I send it. She texts me back in seven seconds flat. (I guess it's not too late.)

22:30 – Go to sleep thinking about the incredible merit I have to partake in this extraordinary chapter of Jewish history – living in the Land and State of Israel. To experience the craziness of this place and the holiness of life here all at once. Can't wait to see what tomorrow brings!

Finding My Home

Jonathan Josephs

> Jonathan is an international jurist, public speaker on cyber-hate, and a member of the Global Forum for Combating Anti-Semitism. He made aliyah from France in 2012, enjoying the fun and the sun of Tel Aviv. Since then, he became vegan, married a kibbutznik, fathered a baby sabra and moved to the 'burbs of Givatayim, living the "Israeli dream".

It was over breakfast that I made the decision that was to change my life. A wet April morning in Montpellier; the TV news was reporting the latest polls for the French presidential elections. Francois Hollande was widely tipped to win by the tightest of margins.

The announcement I was about to make to my parents was not one I had seriously thought through. Truth be told, I had only considered the idea a mere 10 minutes earlier. I had always been impulsive, but what I was about to say took impulsivity to a new level.

"Mum, Dad, I'm going to move to Israel and make aliyah."

The ensuing silence lasted less than a couple of seconds but it felt like a lifetime. How would my parents react? My dad stood up and hugged me. My mum, holding back tears, promptly joined him. In the background, the newsreader reported that the trial of Norwegian mass murderer Anders Breivik had just commenced. My parents were still hugging me, and I had to gently disengage them to get back to my breakfast – baguette spread with Marmite. Born in England but raised in France, my identity has always been somewhat confused.

The next week, I was in contact with the Jewish Agency in Marseille, and started the official process required for aliyah. Hollande was elected French president, and the images of the victory celebrations going on in Paris were of Algerian, Moroccan, and Tunisian flags flying high over the Place de la Bastille.

A few weeks earlier I had been beaten up by a gang of youths in the street in a completely unprovoked attack. I had sustained facial injuries. The gang leader was jailed for violent aggravated assault. A few days later, while waiting for a tram, I was assaulted again by a gang of youths from the bad part of town.

I'm happy to say I made a full recovery from both attacks, but my thoughts did turn to those poor children who were murdered a couple of months earlier in a Jewish school in Toulouse for the simple fact that they were Jewish. I am not optimistic about the future of France, nor for the rest of Europe, for that matter. I no longer feel safe walking around the streets of France.

By the following month, I had gathered all the necessary documents, gone for the official interview, and had my aliyah approved. Then the "is this really happening?" stage kicked in. Did I unthinkingly rush into this process? Definitely. Was I ready for the realities of life in Israel? Probably not. Was I willing to give it the best possible shot? Absolutely.

I said goodbye to my parents, and went through airport security without looking back. The flight was uneventful. I read the papers (the elections in Egypt were in full swing, Greece was collapsing) and tried to learn a few words of Hebrew. I arrived at Ben Gurion late in the evening, as a new immigrant with nothing but three bags and my guitar to my name. The process that began at that momentous breakfast and culminated in my arrival in Tel Aviv had taken a mere three months.

There was nobody to greet me at the airport, nor was I expecting anybody. A large group of well-wishers was waiting to celebrate the arrival of a nice French family who made aliyah on my flight. As they saw me walking past, alone, they grabbed my hands and included me in their party, dancing and hoisting me up and down on a chair.

The taxi driver dropped me off at my friend's apartment in central Tel Aviv. I was to stay on his couch until I found a suitable place to live. The driver barely had time to unload my bags before my friend whisked me off to the nearest pub.

The barman said that the first drink was on the house for all new Israelis. Unwittingly or not, he forgot and charged us anyway. Did I feel guilty buying beer with the grant the government gives to all new immigrants? Not one bit.

My first couple of weeks as an Israeli flashed by. Which was odd, given that I spent most of my time in drab offices, sorting out my national security ID, my health insurance, my bank account, my registration at the Ministry of Absorption, my driver's license … The process was relatively painless, and I was relieved not to encounter any of the red-tape related horrors for which Israeli bureaucracy is famous. There was plenty of time for that to come, I thought.

At my local falafel stall, upon hearing that I just made aliyah, the person next in the queue said he would buy me lunch. This time I didn't have to spend my government money on falafel – the man kept his promise.

Tel Aviv was bustling with tourists, and I felt like one of them. My first month in Israel felt more like an extended holiday than the beginning of a new life. By day, I wandered the streets of Tel Aviv, soaking up the atmosphere. In France, I would have been constantly looking over my shoulder – here, I didn't have to.

One moment particularly stood out. I saw a pensioner

struggling to walk down the street on a hot summer afternoon. A man rushed out of a hair salon and invited him in to sit down and have a glass of water. For some reason, I found the gesture deeply moving – as if that one small kindness revealed the spirit of solidarity that exists between Israelis.

Other gestures were less impressive, such as the constant elbowing I experienced whenever I was waiting patiently in line, like a good Englishman is trained to do. Apparently, solidarity does not extend to queueing.

I had found a job as an in-house lawyer for a technology firm, which was fortunate because I had been spending far too much of my grant on partying, and by the end of the first month I was more or less broke.

On my first day at the office, I turned up in my newly pressed suit, crisp white shirt, and neatly knotted tie and quickly realized I was disastrously overdressed. Israelis wear jeans and polo shirts at work usually – definitely no ties. Luckily, my new colleagues were willing to overlook my sartorial blunder and I was welcomed into the company.

But not by everyone. I had barely been shown to my desk when a man approached, shook my hand, and proceeded to shout at me. I had no idea who he was or what he was going on about. My fairly basic Hebrew wasn't up to the task, but I could definitely tell he wasn't inviting me out to lunch. What could I have done wrong?

Just when I thought he had finished, he went off on another, even louder, shouting bout. I glanced at the administrative assistants who were struggling to hide their giggles. Eventually, they interrupted him, and explained that he had the wrong guy. Apparently, he was supposed to be giving the ear bashing to another new immigrant in the office. A simple, terrifying case of mistaken identity.

I soon learned that, unlike in England or France, where shouting at someone means that you have probably done something pretty bad, in Israel this isn't the case. People seem to relish being shouted at. To reply, you simply shout back in return, only a few decibels louder. Even now, I am amazed when I go to a meeting and hear people yelling at each other as if they were the bitterest enemies, and then see them five minutes later, laughing over a joke at lunch.

The other famed custom of Israelis is their impatience at traffic lights. Israelis have an astute sense of timing and can correctly predict the precise moment the light will turn green. If you do not drive off within the next millisecond, make no mistake, you will get honked at.

I was loving life in Tel Aviv, but one event brought me crashing back to reality. It was the news that a suicide bomber had boarded a bus in Bulgaria and killed seven Israelis. Somehow, I felt personally attacked.

I wanted to share my anger and sadness with my colleagues and expected them to be as outraged as I was. But they didn't seem to be affected. "These things happen" was the normal reply, accompanied by a shrug of the shoulders. Have the sheer number of these attacks over the years desensitized Israelis? Sad songs played on the radio, and life went on.

One month later, I was due to speak at a conference in Berlin on legal measures to combat online antisemitism and Holocaust denial. It was my first trip abroad since I'd made aliyah. When the speaker introduced me as "Jonathan Josephs, from Israel" I felt an intense moment of pride.

To be able to speak on efforts to combat antisemitism in Germany was one thing; doing so as a new citizen of the State of Israel was quite another.

Many immigrants say they can't recall when they started

to feel like a proper Israeli. I can. It was in my fourth month. I was behind a car at a traffic light. The light went green. The car in front didn't immediately drive off. You guessed it. I honked. Israelis up and down the country would have been proud of me.

Soon after, there was the watershed moment when I ordered a beer in Hebrew, and the waitress answered me in Hebrew, instead of English.

I was speaking and understanding more of the language, and at the office, I felt confident enough to give a legal presentation. I wasn't sure whether my colleagues understood me or were just being polite, until I remembered that Israelis aren't known for being polite.

The next evening, as I was driving back from work on the Ayalon motorway, the traffic suddenly screeched to a halt. People were getting out of their cars and lying on the ground. The first rocket attack on Tel Aviv since the Gulf War was in progress.

But I didn't know that. I had turned up the CD player and missed the warning. By that point, I wanted to show everyone what an integrated Israeli I had become. So I proceeded to honk my horn and continued weaving between the stopped cars. It was only when I arrived at home and saw my flatmates sheltering in the stairway that I understood what was happening.

Waiting for the all clear in the bomb shelter was one of my less pleasant Israeli experiences. The elderly woman sheltering next to me saw that I wasn't coping well with the stress and reassured me with a friendly smile and a few kind words. The fact that she was a Holocaust survivor helped put the danger into perspective.

Later, I went down to the grocery store across the street. A few locals from the neighborhood were sitting outside, listening to music, sharing jokes, and drinking beers. I joined them.

I realized that, bombs notwithstanding, I didn't want to be anywhere else.

Returning to my flat, I saw that I parked my car on a yellow line. But I knew I wouldn't get a ticket – the authorities had more important things to deal with, and, besides, we were all united by having survived the rocket attack.

Just before falling asleep, a friend from England phoned. He had heard about the attack. Israel was too dangerous, he told me. I should come back to Europe immediately. I told him, no. This beautiful, vibrant, and lively country had welcomed me with open arms. I was happy to be in Israel.

The next morning, I found a 250 shekel parking ticket stuck under my windshield wiper. I couldn't help laughing. That's when I realized I was home.

Tears of Laughter

Larry David once said, "I'm not an inventor. I'm an improver. I improve things that are broken." Whether it's improvisation, comedy sketch, or stand up, Molly is improving life in Israel one chuckle at a time, with an honest and hilarious view of the Holy Land. She is a comedian, content writer and freelance reporter, not to mention a mother of two. Molly made aliyah in 2005.

I moved to Israel. I made aliyah. And then I got my aliyah name. And it changed me forever. Because it happened to me. It happened.

I grew up in Los Angeles, with the very convenient name (just ask any of my teachers throughout the years who could easily pronounce it without hesitation) Molly Livingstone.

Then I moved to Israel, and that name, I guess, didn't have a kosher ring to it, so they made my last name Levenson.

There's more.

My first name, when pronounced with the Hebrew letters, went from Molly to Muli. It's not a name so much as a sound. When you say it out loud, you might begin choking. Not just from trying to say it, but because you feel bad for me, knowing that this is who I am now. A Muli. Even Word wants to change it. Sorry, spell check, it's not going away.

Because that's who I am now.

As much as I fight the name – you can feel how much I am against it, right? – in some strange way, I have begun to own it. I am this person now.

I came out of the closet. As a Zionist.

It has taken me 10 years of living in Israel, but I finally feel brave enough to say that yes, I am a Zionist. That I love Israel, flaws and all. For her challenges, and people, and for the times she makes me cry, even for no reason, and the laughter and joy she gives me, also for no reason. For the moments of awe. Moments of fear. And the moments in between.

I wasn't raised a Zionist (clearly). I was Jew-*ish*. I knew about apples and honey, and presents on Hanukkah. I understood there was a Jewish Homeland somewhere in the Middle East, but it seemed far away, physically and emotionally. Then Birthright started. And I still didn't go. But then my friend was killed in a bombing in 2002, during the second intifada, at Hebrew University. She loved Israel. And I loved her. So I decided to bite the bullet (maybe even literally) and come to Israel.

I did Birthright. I was in college and it was free. I hiked and I biked. And maybe I fell off the bike too many times... and that was that. I was head over heels – literally – in love with the country. Madly. Deeply. In love. I couldn't get enough.

I moved here. With no real plans. Internship. Finish school. Maybe go to Iraq and be a war correspondent.

But the war was much more at home with me in Israel. War with the language I didn't know. War with a culture I couldn't quite grasp. War with how to eat hummus and pita. Life's simple ways were complicated by a lack of understanding, a passion without reason, and just straight up confusion.

I didn't give up. I think at some point I gave in. I became Muli. I learned the language. I figured out there are no lines, not metaphorically, I mean standing in lines is not a thing (abstract art and elbows). And I own hummus and pita, you should see the way I can wipe down a plate.

I don't know when I made the transition, but somewhere I became more Israeli, from my hand gestures to my dreams (not as in goals and aspirations, more like I started dreaming in Hebrew). I think the most obvious change, and maybe dare I say the healthiest, is how I handle the stress of life. Because life in Israel, if I haven't made it clear yet, is stressful. Yes, the terror is scary. But so is trying to open a bank account.

I think the difference is that terror is more obvious and clear. It happens, it can happen; you know how to deal with it. You know to be afraid of it, and you are. You become prepared, being observant, maybe avoiding certain areas, and pretending you are a Mossad (CIA) agent (or maybe that's just me). But a bank account. You will go to the bank five times. Be told five different things. Bring five different documents. Go through five different strikes. Find they are closed at five different times. And after five months still not have a bank account.

It was times like this as a new immigrant that I felt cultural shock. That I felt regret. That I cried deep into my pillow (walls are thin here). And then, with time, I learned to be more Israeli. More Muli than Molly. Muli would laugh at the fifth time she was told to fax (who faxes things, what's a fax machine) another document. Muli would bring a magazine and understand that she would wait at least an hour to speak to someone, only to find out what a fax machine is. Muli could understand that in the end it would all work out.

Yes, this is a famous saying in Israel, "Yiyeh b'seder," it will be OK. A saying Molly once feared and Muli now embraces. It is the way of the land, and why Israel is actually one of the happiest countries in the world (like there is research that proves that). It has given me the opportunity to find the cup-half-full side of life, and enjoy mistakes as opportunities. I appreciate the moments, instead of calculating the future. In Israel, we understand that future is too long-term and today is all we have. We take with us, in every step, the struggle for the Jewish people to exist, as a religion and as a state. One step at a time.

The Magic of Purim and Aliyah

Jessica Levine Kupferberg

It's one in the morning on Purim, and I finally finished baking hamentashen with my three teen/'tween daughters. This year, in addition to the usual strawberry jam, chocolate chip, and peanut butter and chocolate flavors, we've added a new one to our repertoire in honor of becoming Israelis: Sumsumia, a halva-esque delight made with a sweet sesame and honey paste, serendipity from the Pereg store at Machane Yehuda.

Seven months have now passed since we remade our lives in our homeland. While we still have our "aliyah challenge moments," they are fewer and farther between. Most days, we appreciate that we just get to live here and experience the regular, everyday rhythm of Anglo-Israeli life. We work here, learn here, do laundry here, sweat, cry, play soccer, and cook here. We now eat shakshuka for dinner and toastim for breakfast, have seen Peter Pan fly on a stage in Jerusalem and explored wildflowers and old luminous bell caves on a ditch day from school. We've learned where to shop, who to ask for what, and how to Waze ourselves from here to there. We're just living. In Israel.

While aliyah has had its fair share of heartache and head-aches, to counter some of the frustrations that new olim can face, we heeded one of the best pieces of advice (thanks, Ben!) we received when we made the move: To treat every initial trip to a government office as an exploratory "pilot trip" so when nothing is accomplished, we won't be disappointed. And it's worked. When we have actually achieved success on our first trip to the DMV or Misrad of Whatever & Waiting, we've been pleasantly surprised, and when we haven't, we shrug our shoulders and say, "Pilot trip!"

For each moment of frustration, there is at least one equal and opposite moment of grace, one that really makes you stop and smell the shawarma, the grander little moments where your Jewish heart gets lodged in your throat and you just say: Thank G-d. And Purim here is certainly one of them.

While we enjoyed many wonderful Purim celebrations in our old-country home of La Jolla, California, we've discovered that Israel takes the party to a whole new level. The one day holiday gets super-sized into two weeks of festivities as stores everywhere peddle masks and wands, baskets and candies. The malls have their own Purim stations and the schools each have a shuk Purim with food and games for the kids.

But my favorite activity so far took place the last day before Purim break, when we experienced the Adeloyada Parade. This is where all the school-age kids don a bevy of creative, vibrant costumes and parade down the streets of our town, an exercise that's repeated in cities and settlements all over Israel.

While many parents don't attend, as a still-fresh immigrant celebrating our first Purim as Israelis, I couldn't help myself. I attempted not to embarrass my kids as I paparazzied them with their friends to capture the festive feeling. The kids were bursting with pride and excitement as they laughed at each other's costumes and compared notes on the *mishloach manot* baskets they prepared for one another. My daughters, as the new kids, were afraid to wear costumes that were too creative or different, but looked great as a mime, a magician, and a home-made "WhatsApp." Their schoolmates were dazzling; smiling superheroes, produce from the seven species, a pre-teen Aroma waitress, and a sparkly rainbow all heralded Purim together. My niece was a homemade laundry machine and one girl was even an entire birthday party as she lugged a long cardboard table on her shoulders, complete with a birthday cake, hat and balloons.

And then there were all the little soldiers toting mini plastic weapons. Seeing "guns" carried by 8-year-olds is still really jarring. This certainly wasn't our experience in American day school, where the rules declare, "No pretend weapons of any kind may be used with your costume." Here, we witnessed two shrunken soldiers cruising in an Israeli army jeep fashioned out of a cardboard box and driven Flintstone style to the parade. Another cardboard box was transformed into a tank, ready to guard the Jewish state. I reminded myself about the cultural differences here, where these kids, including my own, will evolve into real soldiers one day and must be comfortable holding, or even using, real guns. There were girl Mossad agents and SWAT teams and policemen. While Bibi was busy prepping for his much talked about speech, these kids were already preparing to ensure that the Jewish state remains secure in the future.

I admit I felt a bit foolish, but couldn't stifle the tears of pride as we marched down the street while the gleaming Judean Hills and little costume-clad gan children served as our spectators. The music truck followed along, lights flashing as it blared the tunes I first learned in pre-school in a land far way. And here I was, walking with my kids, celebrating the joyous survival of the Jewish people, a feeling so much more powerful this year after sitting in a bomb shelter shortly after our arrival this past summer. All this as Bibi was just hours away from warning Congress and the world about the perils of a nuclear Iran nearby.

As we marched, my 11-year-old (thankfully not ashamed to be seen with me yet) turned to me, a broad grin materializing like a rabbit from under her magician's hat, and she marveled,

"At least here, on Purim people don't look at us like we're weirdos." And she was right. In America, even I felt self-conscious in our old neighborhood when I'd venture out in the middle of March, Halloween nowhere in sight, dressed like a Slurpee or Miss Piggy; a moment that used to remind us that we were outsiders there. Abracadabra, she understood the magic of aliyah: of living in a place where we truly belong.

10 Years

Hilary Faverman

A content marketer by trade and a pie-baking, sausage-making sarcastic mama by nature, Hilary hesitantly moved to Israel from Wisconsin ten years ago and today divides her time between wrangling her four children and attempting to grasp the Israeli fascination with fried chickpeas. You can find her published on Kveller and The Times of Israel as well as her own blog, www.HilaryFaverman.com. Hilary made aliyah in 2004.

As of today, I've been in Israel for 10 years. When I tell people that the first seven were the toughest, they laugh. But I am so not kidding.

This is a hard place to get used to. Especially when you arrive with no linguistic, historical or cultural knowledge, and get pregnant within four minutes. Then, you find yourself alone in an Arab-Jewish neighborhood (I wanted to be open-minded) with a screaming newborn (maternal instinct triumphs over sleep deprivation, right?). I was wrong on both counts.

My six-figure career got me nowhere, as limited liability lectures and union negotiations were worthless in the framework of an entirely different legal system.

My flippant humor was suddenly inconsequential, as it's hard to be charismatic when your Wisconsin Hebrew school language skills amount to "Notebook. Pencil. My teacher is pretty." (Thanks, Mrs. Schwartz.)

My chameleonic ability to make friends anywhere and everywhere was effectively tossed aside when I realized that Anglo Jerusalemites categorize potential friends in one of several different boxes: bandana, wig, scarf, jean skirt, egalitarian minyan. Treif is not one of the boxes, however, so even my million dollar smile didn't earn me a community.

So why did I stay through seven years of difficulty, and how did I come out happy on the other side?

Those are two entirely separate questions. First, why did I stay? Anyone who has met my husband knows about The Dimple Factor. Picture Vin Diesel with dimples the size of nails. He also happens to be one of the most upstanding people I've ever met, and I was in HR for 10 years. I've met a lot of people.

He wanted to be here, and I wanted him to be happy. It's not necessarily the decision everyone would make, but when his company tried to relocate us to New Jersey (all expenses paid + a promotion), I was the one who declined. Pirate's Booty and Target just didn't make the cut.

We were initially here for a year, on a trial basis. I was the only one on the Nefesh B'Nefesh flight who shed tears of hand-wringing anxiety rather than of joy. The first year was an emotional roller coaster of ulpan, pregnancy, struggling through an emergency cesarean and the feeling of failure surrounding both the natural birth I had envisioned and the ideal newborn mother I had anticipated being.

Those first five years showed small wins:

We bought an apartment. It was in a Sefardi, old-school, neighbors-know-your-business neighborhood because that's what we could afford. Considering we had moved from Abu Tor, where rocks were thrown at my stroller, puppies were tortured behind my building, two robberies rocked our sense of security, and Hamas flags were paraded regularly through the neighborhood at 4 a.m., this was an improvement. One of the local women helped me make kubeh. She also stopped by with meat every time we turned on the BBQ, telling us she'd be back in 30 minutes and not to burn it. Ah, Katamonim.

Never having been required to cook before, (I lived in Manhattan and worked 60 hours/week! Two words: Take. Out.) I learned how to cook in earnest. And bake pie. One-handed. (After the first newborn came two more, and I was getting the hang of things.) I learned that the artistry which struck my grandmother and my sister but had conspicuously skipped me, much to my disappointment, could manifest itself through food. I began making elaborate meals and struggled to invite guests to dine in our non-kosher home. Fail.

I began working in an industry where I flourished. I was promoted. Several times. Within three years, I was a major ingredient in the financial success of the company and co-workers and colleagues alike began to know my name. Professionally, I was growing and things were looking up.

My beg list (things I begged people to bring from the States) gradually got shorter. I got used to Osem ketchup and no longer shelled out the extra shekels for Heinz. I began to go to the grocery store alone, after a year or two of dragging my beloved with me to battle what I called "the white stuff section." (I still don't know the difference between labaneh and eshel, and I don't care.)

My oldest started first grade at the most wonderful school. I fought tooth and nail to get her accepted, and at the culmination of that process, I was not only triumphant, I understood that in Israel, "No" simply means "Not yet." And freshly baked cookies go a long way toward moving from "not yet" to "maybe soon" and finally to "Okay, just stop stalking us. Bring more cookies."

That year, we determined that living in a heavily religious

(and growing more extreme by the minute) city with three kids in a two-bedroom apartment was not viable long-term. Go ahead, though, and attempt to sell an 80 meter apartment that is 40 meters on paper. What in the world does that mean? It took me a while to understand, but it seems that the legalities normally attributed to building or expanding a property didn't apply to the "metzukah" (poor) neighborhood of the Katamonim until we wanted to sell our apartment. Then, they applied. We spent over a year legalizing the expansions done on our apartment before we bought it, and another year getting permission from our neighbors (okay, going around our neighbors' blockages in court) to build an extra room. We finally sold and effectively bought our ticket out of the city.

Enter my favorite two hashtags: #MoshavLife and #BackyardPoultry. Go ahead. Facebook them. We moved to a very small, reasonably quaint, mixed (religious and secular) moshav about half an hour from Jerusalem. I couldn't walk to buy milk, but I could see wildlife from my deck (and I had a deck!).

I began to find local friends who didn't care where I went to shul, or if I went to shul. They didn't care whether or how I covered my hair, or how treif-y my kitchen was. These were English speakers who identified with my "Jerusalem Refugee" status.

I started to notice other things, as well. Although I've lived for significant periods in New York, San Francisco, and Boston (Never live in Boston. I repeat: Never. Live. There.), I am a small-town girl at heart, hailing from a Milwaukee suburb. Yes, there are Jews in Milwaukee.

Where I grew up, about half a mile from our house sits the local elementary school. Around the school is a curved, tree-lined street which guides visitors and residents alike into our mostly hidden, working-class neighborhood. Every fall, the trees on that street sway in the wind and turn golden, and then vibrantly orange. It's really a trademark of the neighborhood. Long after I'd left the area for college, and Wisconsin altogether, to begin my career, I returned every Thanksgiving to the awaiting trees, welcoming me home as the last leg of my journey. Those trees always represented home for me; the feeling of wholeness, acceptance, and being rooted.

My tiny moshav is across the highway from a (slightly) larger community, where the local (ridiculously overpriced) supermarket sits, as well as the elementary school. I hosted 25 guests this year on Thanksgiving, like I always do, for traditional turkey, fixings, and pie. This year, as I was heading to pick up my kids from school on Thanksgiving Day (can you imagine the audacity of these teachers, holding school on Thanksgiving?), I noticed that the entrance to the community was lined with trees. The road curved. The leaves rustled in the breeze. And they were yellowing with the season.

I stopped my car.

I'd lived there for three years. Why had I never noticed the identical characteristics of that road and my childhood landmark? As unexplained, unannounced tears fell from my face, it hit me: It wasn't the trees that triggered this response. It was the feeling. I felt at home. It was only then I noticed the parallel, because my emotional compass had been missing the feeling of belonging for so long.

After 10 years, three kids, two jobs, and a community I cannot live without... I am welcome. And I am home. Happy Aliyah-versary to me.

The Five Stages of Aliyah

Jen Maidenberg

> A New Jersey native, Jen is a freelance writer, editor, and
> mother of three who lives on Kibbutz Hannaton. Her cre-
> ative nonfiction column, "My Time, Your Place" is published
> bi-monthly in District Lit, an online journal of writing and
> art based in Washington, DC. Jen received her MA from
> the Shaindy Rudoff Graduate Program in Creative Writing.
> She was recently named a finalist for the *Ruminate Magazine*
> Spiritual Nonfiction Prize. Jen made aliyah in 2010.

My aliyah is closing in on three years.

Three years of braving Hebrew.

Three years of navigating bureaucracy.

Three years of saying, *"Slicha, ani olah chadasha."*

I often say I am so thankful we made aliyah in 2010 – in the
days of Google Translate, Eden Teva, social media, and other
modern amenities that have surely made my transition easier
than my predecessors'.

I can't really complain.

Except I can.

Because that's what complainglos do.

Except I don't see it as complaining – I never did. I call it
processing. I call it cultural exchange. I call it the third stage of
the five stages of aliyah.

The first is joy: "We're here! We're really here! Israel is
AMAZING."

The second is confusion: "What? I didn't think it would be this hot/hard/expensive here in Israel. It wasn't this hot/hard/expensive the last three times I visited."

The third stage – the phase in which complaining usually occurs in excess – is comparison: "I don't understand how they don't have organic chicken in this country. They have organic eggs. Where is the organic chicken?"

The fourth stage is letting go, sometimes utterly and completely. I recently passed through this phase. In fact, I'm still with one leg in it. In this phase, you decide to truly be Israeli. You go whole kosher hog. You make assumptions about what it means to fit in – to be Israeli – and act upon it:

1. You yell back at the woman in the grocery store parking lot who calls you an idiot because you're actually waiting for someone to exit a spot before you enter.

2. You get into a heated debate with your son's math teacher about why it's her fault he failed the test, not his.

3. You turn *"Makolet Day"* into *"Makolet Summer."*

4. You show up 15 minutes late to every meeting, on purpose, even if you are genetically predisposed to show up early.

5. You allow the neighbor's constantly unleashed dog to lick your leg even though you know you'll break out in hives. *"Ain mah la'asot,"* you tell yourself. "Dogs will be dogs."

You hang out in stage four for a while – at least I have – and you pat yourself on the back. "Look at me. I'm such an Israeli. I'm *totally* fitting in here. I'm gonna make it after all!"

You tell your co-workers about how you beat the system this way or that way. You share your success stories in broken Hebrew with your Israeli-born girlfriends and they smile sweetly at you. You feel part of the crowd. You feel as if everything is going to be alright.

The fifth stage in any trauma or transition is typically acceptance. This is the phase in which we have processed our circumstances; we have acknowledged our reality; and now life must continue.

But acceptance is often confused with the notion of "everything being okay."

Everything is *not* okay here in Israel.

Israel is no different from any other country (or person) in that there are problems, there are challenges, and there is always room for improvement.

I accept that I live here, and I accept the reality of the culture here. I accept the fact that gas is high and availability of organic, nut-free, natural products is low.

But I don't necessarily accept the Israeli version of me that I became in stage four when I practiced "letting go." I don't want to be her. I won't.

There are parts of that self I like and admire – parts I want to keep, parts I am grateful to Israel for. It's only by living here that those parts were able to bubble to the surface and were cultivated.

I like that I'm less rigid with my children. I like that I am now able to stand up for myself – out loud and vocally – when the situation calls for it. I like that I am more compassionate and forgiving since living in a small kibbutz community; since living on top of people who live life differently from how I do.

But on the other hand, I don't want to be someone who yells. I don't want to be someone who shows up late. I don't want to be someone who speaks nastily. I don't want to ever say, "*Ain ma la'asot.*"

I like being someone who speaks kindly (or, at the very least, works hard at speaking kindly). And I want my children to speak that way, too. I want to show respect to my fellow human beings by following through on what I say I am going to do. If I indicate

I am going to be somewhere at 8 a.m., for instance, I want to be there at 8 a.m. Because I believe it says something about my character and my commitment. And if I have a conflict with my son's teacher, I want it to be a civilized discussion, in which we come to an agreed upon conclusion.

I don't want my kids to toss trash on the ground or make "*sini*" eyes or refer to particular problems as "the fault of *ha'aravim*." These are all cultural realities here – and they aren't ones I am going to comply with just to fit in.

Stage five may be acceptance, but it need not be, "everything is okay here." Surely, it includes acknowledging cultural differences, recognizing regional challenges, and understanding that long-term cultural change requires much more effort than it takes to complain or blog. Long-term cultural change requires a tipping point – it requires enough people wanting the change to happen. Whether the change is coexistence, speaking more nicely, or earth-friendly legislation.

Any good Israeli would tell you that you're a *friar* if you don't try something before you buy it. So I'm offering up myself to try.

Try me. The non-Israeli parts of me.

Before rushing to call me an Anglo or "too American," see how my non-Israeli parts suit you.

The showing up on time, the talk of mindfulness, the love and care of the planet, the criticism of artificial food coloring – try it.

Try it, and then maybe … buy it.

You might like it even better than *Big Brother.*

Angry Anglo-Bloggers, Why Can't We All Just Get Along?

Benji Lovitt

Since making aliyah in 2006, comedian Benji has performed for audiences around the world including Hillels, Birthright Israel, and Jewish Federations. His perspectives on life in Israel have been featured on Israeli television and radio and in publications such as *USA Today*, *Time* magazine, Huffington Post, The Times of Israel, and more. His annual Yom Ha'atzmaut list of things he loves about Israel has developed a huge following. Benji is a member of the ROI Community.

Once upon a time, 45 bajillion blog posts were written about olim, their complaints, and a partridge in a pear tree. In our immediate-reaction, "look, two things happened within three hours … it's a meme!" society, people began talking about the internet's back-and-forth between "*olim hadashim,*" "*olim vatikim,*" and their upcoming bout at Wrestlemania 28. (Main event: Hollywood Hulk Hogan vs. Shmuel Goldfish, loser leaves town and moves to Galilee as part of Nefesh B'Nefesh's "Go North" campaign.)

Complaints ranged from "Living here is more difficult than I expected because of false expectations" to "We need to take a long, hard look at how to keep human capital here."

Responses in blog posts and talkbacks ranged from "You can always leave" and "You forfeit the right to complain when you move here" to "If you dare criticize this country, I will shove a 10-foot mezuzah down your throat." OK, so I made that one up.

Whoa. Don't people have less combative things to do? Like Pinterest?

What are we even talking about anymore? The conversation went from addressing specific complaints to the very right of people to complain, with what was perceived as, accurately or not, *olim hadashim* in one corner and *olim vatikim* in the other. I could only read so many of these before wondering when a different voice was going to jump in. Can I represent *olim beinoni'im* (or perhaps just myself)? Because G-d knows this part of the world needs as much mediation as possible.

Could it be that there's no actual phenomenon here, but that, instead, it's just a function of the internet? Everyone knows that blogs and sites like Twitter and Facebook give people a microphone, and that it's much easier to express yourself (read: complain) now than in the old days.

Seriously, how did people make aliyah before the internet existed?

I would love to read the unwritten blog posts of yesteryear. I mean, have you ever heard the horror stories that olim from the '70s and '80s tell to elicit a reaction? Holy hell, can anyone confirm whether or not they're even true?

"When I moved here 30 years ago, it took three months to get a phone line installed. And you had to give blood before they'd even come to your house."

"Omigod, you had to give blood!? That sounds HORRIBLE!"

"TOTALLY. And, if you wanted to switch banks, you had to first withdraw all your money, and then the bank you were leaving would give you 613 lashings."

Let's review, shall we?

One blogger wrote:

"To voluntarily immigrate somewhere and then subsequently complain about the culture into which you wish to integrate is fairly audacious. In Israel, *zeh mah she'yesh*. This is what you signed up for, kids."

I don't know about you guys, but I didn't sign up for an 80-year-old Polish grandmother elbowing me in the small of my back while cutting in line. How was I supposed to see that coming when I was singing outdated David Broza songs at Young Judaea summer camp and eating nasty falafel I thought was tasty? WHAT WERE WE THINKING? Oh right, we weren't. We were teenagers. But how many Anglo olim would come if they knew the whole truth? Definitely fewer. Maybe we should start advertising the real Israel so people can know what they really signed up for.

Another wrote:

"There is a disturbing new phenomenon afoot, one that I have dubbed 'complainglos'; that is, Anglos who seek to ease the difficulties of absorption and assimilation by bashing everything about life in Israel."

Well, I certainly hope they're not bashing *everything* about Israel. Yes, Anglos complain, but does anyone actually believe this is a new phenomenon? If complaining *has* increased over the years, the only people who'd have the perspective to recognize it are those who have been here for decades.

The Sages said that as long as birds are of a particular feather, they will flock together and complain about worms (or something like that). Having a community of fellow English-speakers provides a support system. However, it comes hand in hand with the motivation to complain.

I even found an angry rant from one oleh complaining about Israelis violently pushing people out of the way to board the Egged 405 line, with the guy changing the words of "David

Melech Yisrael" to expletives. Oh wait, you're saying that was me five years ago? Moving on…

Is this place awesome? Yes. Are Israelis the hottest Jews ever? Yes. But, let's be honest, a lot of things need fixing and anyone who's paying attention knows it. Maybe it's the government, maybe it's different groups having too much or too little power.

New generations of *complainglos* are like *The Lion King*: It's the circle of life. Except that instead of singing lions we have Westerners wondering how many times they have to call Orange without getting hung up on.

During my senior year of college (right around the time of the Ben-Gurion administration), I wrote a psychology thesis on ethnic humor. I ran an experiment confirming what we already know: A member of an in-group can make jokes that a non-member cannot get away with. For instance, a black guy can tell a black joke but a white guy can't. (Fortunately, I can get away with it, seeing as I'm dark on the inside and white on the outside. They don't call me "reverse krembo" for nothing.)

Israelis (and when I say "Israelis" I include us olim) can tolerate a lot more criticism from people who actually live here than from those who don't. It's that whole "you can't beat up my little brother – only *I* can beat him up" thing.

Most people who live here will let criticism from their fellow aliyah brothers and sisters slide because they know that they're on the same team, members of the same proverbial family. They know that the complainer has decided to cast his lot with the Jewish people in Israel and shares the same strong emotional investment in this country.

Here's a little secret that's actually not a secret to anyone who's followed my humor for the last few years: For the better part of 364 days out of the year, I complain, and I complain too much. So why don't Israelis or *olim vatikim* tell me to shut my krembo-hole? Presumably because I have a sense of humor about it and bring a smile to people's faces, highlighted by my annual critique-free Yom Ha'atzmaut list. What people don't know is that I've also been toying with the idea of making a "sixty-whatever things I hate about Israel" list. Why haven't I done it? Because if it fell into the hands of those who don't really know me it could lead them to think I don't really want to be here.

In the wise words of one of the aforementioned bloggers:

"It does us no good to cling to the comparisons. We are here for no other reason than that we want to be here."

He's right: You shouldn't compare between countries. It serves little purpose, and it's frustrating. And, to be fair, I'm the first to admit that I'm poor at taking this advice.

Olim hadashim, it will get easier. *Olim vatikim*, the newbies need your help, inspiration, and understanding. Do your best Mr. Miyagi and pass on your infinite wisdom, provided it doesn't require anyone to paint both sides of a fence.

Let us all enjoy this wonderful country together in peace and harmony. Anybody want a *hafuch*?

My First Aliyahversary:
An Ode to Israel

Ariella Siegel

Ariella is a wanderer, traveler, and seeker of truth. She made aliyah in July 2015 after completing her master's degree in religious studies at Florida International University in Miami, FL. She is a writer and social media manager for an incredible company called DEEP (www.deep.it) and is currently living and enjoying life immensely in Tel Aviv.

Growing up in America, we were taught to protect ourselves. *My* house, *my* family, *my* things. Be wary of people you don't know (stranger danger). Don't ride your bike outside the neighborhood. Don't look people in the eye, don't let strangers in your house, don't leave your door unlocked. People can't be trusted, you must fend for yourself, take care of yourself, protect yourself.

One of the reasons I love Israel is because, to me, as an Israeli Jew, it feels like we're all in it together, even when we're fighting with each other. We're all participating in this crazy experiment called Israel, we're all figuring it out as we go along, and we're all family. Sometimes, family can get on your nerves and drive you insane, always sticking their noses into your business. The same goes for Israel. It's like living in a country of Jewish mothers who think they know better than you. It's not unusual for someone to give you feedback on whether your kid is wearing enough clothes in the winter, or to ask how much money you make, or how much you pay for your apartment, or why you're not married yet.

Israelis (in my general experience) are often loud, pushy, have zero shame, are a little cuckoo, and can be fairly impatient. On the other hand, they are ridiculously kind, very loving, will tell you the truth, and never sugarcoat whatever it is that they think or feel. They get emotional very quickly, but then they get over it really quickly as well.

Family, community, and connection are so important to people here. The dads are hands-on in a way I've never seen in any other country. Jewish holidays and simchas are built-in excuses for families and friends to meet, to bond, to eat, to catch up. Israelis are creative, entrepreneurial, adventurous, and don't give a crap what you think. While customer service is lacking (understatement of the century), if someone's in a bad mood, they'll just be in a bad mood. They don't waste energy on faking it, or pretending to be nice (although sometimes that would be a welcome change!).

You have to admire the audacity and authenticity of the people here. I speak about Israelis because they are a product of this great country, of what 68 years of outrageous courage, enormous vision and a boatload of hard work can create. I had a taxi driver once who came to Israel from Lebanon and lived in a tent at a time when there was no actual housing (or roads or infrastructure) here. His father helped build some of the first roads in Tel Aviv, when all there was was sand. Which other country in the world, that is democratic and (mostly) functioning, can say they've accomplished so much in such a short amount of time?

And after almost a year of aliyah, I also love Israel because of who it has turned me into. As an Israeli, I'm more generous. I'm more go-with-the-flow, less structured, less planned (not my choice, but a necessity). I'm more willing to open my heart and my home to people. I trust more, I feel safer, I feel more at home, more like myself. I feel braver and more assertive and happier. I feel challenged, and then triumphant after overcoming those challenges (if you've ever had a successful phone call with Bezek, you'll know what I'm talking about). I'm able to get mad more easily, and let it go just as quickly. I make a mean shakshuka and can haggle the hell out of a salesperson at the shuk.

Israel has sharpened some edges and softened others, as I often say. I am grateful for my first year as an Israeli citizen, and excited and hopeful about living the rest of my life here.

The "Aha!" Moment

Tamar Field-Gersh

Tamar spent seven years as program director of The Tiyul, a summer program for Jewish teens run through the 92nd St Y in NYC. The Tiyul's unique focus was volunteering, environmental education and leadership building. She is currently the program coordinator for Holy Land Spirit, a unique musical and spiritual experience for Christians visiting Israel. When Tamar is not coordinating or organizing something cool, you can find her on the beach at sunset with her four outrageously adorable kids and hubby. Tamar made aliyah in 2004.

You know those "Aha!" moments we all have at some point in our lives? The kind that Oprah Winfrey always talks about? Kind of like, "Aha! It hit me! I want to go back to school to be an acupuncturist!" Or, "Aha! This relationship is *so* not working. I'm out of here!" Well, I'm pretty sure that every oleh and olah has had one of those moments when it becomes completely clear that it's time to uproot everything you know and move life over to that teeny tiny country that requires a magnifying glass to see on a map, where the summers are so hot that they make Bikram yoga seem like a dive in a pool of ice in the Arctic.

As for me, I had my "Aha!" moment when I came to Israel during my junior year of high school and attended the Alexander Muss High School in Israel program, aka AMHSI.

But let me back up for a moment and share with you that my relationship with Israel started way before AMHSI. I was one of those Jewish kids who came to Israel all the time growing up. My grandparents, aunt, uncle, and cousins (basically my mom's entire family) lived in Israel. We spent many Hanukkah vacations, and of course all the family celebrations boarding a plane and making our way to the land flowing with Milky and Bissli, at least that's what it was to a little American girl visiting Grandma in her apartment in Jerusalem. I created so many childhood memories there that now, whenever I drive with my own kids down Palmach Street in Jerusalem, where my grandparents use to live, I can see the ghosts of my grandparents walking home from shul on Shabbat. My grandfather clutching his beautiful multi-colored tallit bag and my grandmother holding onto his other arm. And to smell my grandmother's cooking, I just have to roll down the car window and inhale.

Though I was a frequent visitor to Israel as a kid and then teenager, I actually kept Israel far away from my heart. This is my grandparents' Israel. This is my parents' Israel. She does not belong to me. This is the place I have to come to for our family vacations, instead of going to Disneyland or Hawaii like my school friends; where I have to spend ten days frantically running around visiting old relative after old relative. Sometimes I wondered why my parents wanted to take us so often to a place that was filled with so many bombs and terrorists. Why couldn't they take us, just once, to Disneyland? Of course, falafel and Coca-Cola t-shirts in Hebrew were also cool, but I would have exchanged Israel for a trip to carefree Miami any day.

So you're probably wondering what it was that brought me to move my life to Israel. That's where my "Aha!" moment comes in, of course. It came while I was a student at AMHSI, as I was sitting on a wooden bench outside the Golan winery taking it all in after having done a little wine tasting with my classmates (which the school allowed back then, and, I admit, for sure could have helped that "Aha!" moment come about). I took a deep breath, looked around at the incredibly beautiful land surrounding me, and started to tear up. After spending five life-changing months learning the ins and outs of Jewish and Israeli history, it hit me big. This was my history and I wanted to be a part of it. I needed to be a part of it. Israel, for the first time in my life, was *my* Israel. I knew then and there that I would one day move my life to Israel.

Of course, most "Aha!" moments are full of dreamy and exhilarating emotion. And mine was no exception. But I am also a type-A personality, an over-practical over-thinker, and once I dried those emotional tears, my next thought, though I was only 16 years old, was, "Oh, shit. This is *not* going to be easy."

So, ten years later, with that "Aha!" moment still stuck in my mind and guiding my steps, I made aliyah with my husband (who eventually became a teacher at AMHSI, funny how karma works, huh?). For the first time in my life, I found my heart deeply connecting to a place I can call home. But, like I predicted ten years earlier, it wasn't all going to be easy. Let me tell you about it.

We came with Nefesh b'Nefesh, who are simply amazing as they try to prepare you for every challenge and mishap you may encounter. But, naturally, they can't prepare you for everything, so no one ever tells you as you board that plane that this could be the end of ever feeling like you fully belong anywhere. You might have two passports now but you really have a passport to nowhere. Why? Because you will never really feel like a "true" Israeli, and you will never again feel like a real American.

Shit! Or shall I say *"sheet!"* because I am (kind of) Israeli now, right?

So here I am living my dream in my homeland. But, here, I am not fully Israeli. I am the one driving my kids to school blasting Rusted Root while my horrified kids beg me to turn it off as we approach the final turn to their school (turning it down isn't good enough). I am the one who makes them PB&J sandwiches when I can't think of what else to make for their 10 o'clock snack/lunch. Is it a snack? Is it lunch? See! I'm not fully Israeli! I am the one serving fruit smoothies to my kids' playdates instead of Coke. (Actually – maybe that one is just a hippy thing. Can't blame being an olah on everything.) I am the one who takes an hour to respond to my kids' teachers when they want to know if I can bring in a special dish for a holiday coming up. Not because I don't have an answer, but because I need to spellcheck my response multiple times and check in with my kids to make sure what I wrote makes sense so as not to, God forbid, embarrass my poor kids once again.

On the flip side, during all my trips to the U.S. since making aliyah, I feel like I never lived a day in that country. As my in-laws drive us around, my eyes are fixated out the window as we pass humungous house after more humongous house and manicured lawn after more elaborately manicured lawn. (Since we're talking about lawns, can someone explain to me why Americans have the biggest, greenest, grassy lawns, yet there is never anyone outside playing on them? Where are all the children?) When I go into a store at the mall, I run into a quiet corner, scared of the overly nice workers trying to make chit-chat with me and providing over-the-top customer service. (Why are they asking me so many questions? Why are they trying to help me so much? Help!) As I speak to friends that I have left behind, I find it hard to make a full sentence without naturally throwing in Hebrew words here and there. They are sweet and nice and pretend they understand, but I know they have no idea. They can't. I might possess two passports, but, really, I have citizenship in only one crazy island called "Oleh-land" where you speak this mish-mosh language called Hebrish, to ensure that no one can really ever understand you again.

But I will finish by saying this: For some completely crazy and totally insane reason, it all kind of works. I might have a ticket to nowhere, but I wouldn't change it for anything. I may be neither fully Israeli nor truly American anymore, but I know I have started the process for the next generations, *my* next generations, to feel fully 100% part of their people in their land. I know that I have made the right move towards joining *my* people, being *in* the story, and living and loving *my* Israel.

I Have No Other Country

Laura Ben-David

Laura is a marketing consultant, photographer, and social media activist. Originally from New York, she started writing when she made aliyah from Florida and has never stopped. A popular writer and speaker, Laura's subjects of choice include Israel, aliyah and social media – and sometimes all three at once. She made aliyah in 2002.

You know those things that stir the deeply intense, raw emotions that Zionism inspires within us? Singing "HaTikvah." Watching the movie *Exodus*. Finding an unexpected El Al plane anywhere in the world. Hearing the Yom Hazikaron siren. Seeing IDF soldiers doing, well, just about anything; especially at a formal IDF ceremony... I am particularly susceptible to these emotional triggers; they are no less powerful after more than a dozen years of living in Israel. Perhaps, in fact, they are more powerful.

Attending my first *tekes siyum,* or basic training completion ceremony at the Michve Alon IDF military base, I expect to be moved. And I am. Known for its educational programs, Michve Alon is the first stop for many of the thousands of lone soldiers who come to Israel from all over the world to serve in the IDF; most of whom make aliyah and stay. At Michve Alon, they have basic training along with very intensive Hebrew ulpan to build up their Hebrew language skills. And upon completion of the three-month training (and perhaps one or two other times along the way) there is a *tekes*.

Arriving at the very start of the program, I am stunned at the vastness of the field that hundreds and hundreds of soldiers, standing in formation, are waiting to march onto. I pull out my camera as I spot James, our cousin and our very own lone soldier, the one whose presence brought us to this army base in the north of Israel. Immediately, the music starts, and the soldiers all march in, unit by unit, grinning broadly.

As I take in the proceedings, I gaze at the faces of these hundreds of new soldiers, clearly immigrants from all over the world. I look proudly at the many Israeli flags waving above them in the early evening breeze, bright blue and gleaming white. The sun slowly dips behind the westerly mountains casting a wonderful golden glow. The band is playing "Jerusalem of Gold." I am crying.

Ceremonies can be long and boring; filled with speeches and more than enough pomp and circumstance. One might imagine that the strict discipline of the army would render a ceremony that much more rigid. I know I speak for just one ceremony, but, really, think about all the Israelis you know. The only time I imagine you will get thousands of Israelis standing at attention, silent and motionless, is during the Memorial Day and Holocaust Day sirens. And then it's only for a maximum of two minutes.

The guests are relaxed, the soldiers slightly less so. My camera is clicking away as I try to capture the excitement; the timelessness; the immense pride on every soldier's face. Not just the soldiers, but their officers. And their families. And guests from the local kibbutz that came to show support. And the Nefesh B'Nefesh Lone Soldiers Program team who come to every… single… ceremony. It doesn't get old. Not ever.

Now the soldiers do something remarkable. They are down on their knees, and a soldier stands and calls out words that are the title of a very popular Israeli folk song: *"Ein li eretz acheret!"*

Suddenly an officer shouts, "English!" and a soldier from America stands at attention and translates, "I have no other country!"

The officer shouts, "French!" and the line is repeated in French. Then Spanish. Russian. German. Italian. Chinese. Finnish. Ukrainian. Amharic. Kuki. Each line is received with deep applause since everyone, soldiers and guests alike, understands the commitment and sacrifice that lies behind the decision of every foreign-born soldier, who was not born with the obligation to serve, but rather chose it.

The officer shouts, "Arabic!" An Arab-Israeli soldier stands up and calls out the translation in Arabic to thunderous applause. We think nothing can surprise us more . . . until the officer calls out, "Yiddish!" A bearded, young religious soldier stands and recites his line to equally resounding applause.

Clearly the symbolism of the final two languages is planned. And serves its purpose well. Arabic and Yiddish are spoken by two rather opposite segments of Israeli society: Arabs and ultra-Orthodox Jews. While they are actually from Israel, as opposed to most of the other soldiers at the ceremony, they traditionally do not serve in the army. In that way, the Arabic and Yiddish speaking soldiers have much more in common with the rest of the soldiers then you might have thought . . .

You see, they, too, left their comfort zone and made a choice: they chose Israel.

This is What Happens When You Try to Transplant an American Holiday

Tzippy Levy

> Depending on your perspective, Tzippy was either born an adult or will never really successfully become one. She made aliyah in 2005 from New Jersey and is currently living in Jerusalem with her husband and three children.

I don't really celebrate Thanksgiving in Israel. I don't object to it, I just don't do it. I mean, I like the food and all, but Thanksgiving for me was always basically an excuse to drink eggnog and to see specific family members. Since they don't sell eggnog in Israel, and anyway as an adult I can make it anytime I want, and those family members whom I would see on Thanksgiving are in America…

Well, no. Actually, I did do Thanksgiving that one time.

Friday morning, November 17, 2006. My second November in Israel since making aliyah, my first since getting married. I'm living in a basement apartment in Nachlaot, Jerusalem – a tiny two-room flat whose kitchen is smaller than its bathroom and which suffers from an issue that Israelis euphemistically refer to as "moisture." (In English we call this "mold.") It causes the paint on the walls in the affected areas to peel and flake, and I often find pieces of ceiling in my dust piles when sweeping.

My sister, the Thanksgivophile, is visiting, and we've planned on a Thanksgiving Shabbat. I bought canned pumpkin and found a recipe for pareve pumpkin pie (not an easy feat, by the way), and my mom has emailed us her recipes for stuffing (which, let's be honest, is the real reason to eat a turkey to begin with) and cranberry-apple kugel, as well as instructions for roasting a turkey.

"Did you order a turkey?" my sister asks me.

Order . . . a turkey? Is that a thing? Isn't a turkey just basically a chicken, only bigger, and filled with stuffing? Don't you just go to the store and buy them?

"No, I didn't," I respond, "but we're going to the shuk. You can get anything in the shuk."

Machane Yehuda, the popular open-air market in down-town Jerusalem, is a seven-minute walk from my apartment. And apparently, you can get anything there, although finding a whole turkey may necessitate going around to ten different butchers until you find someone who has an entire frozen twelve-pound turkey.

We bring the thing home, and the three of us (my sister, my husband, and myself) gather around the turkey to decide upon the next step.

"You can cook it frozen, right?"

I've cooked chickens frozen before. And, after all, isn't a tur-key just basically a chicken, only bigger? And filled with stuffing?

Except then I remember an email my mother sent the night before to wish us luck. The email includes this line:

If you're you're using a frozen turkey, you've already got it defrosting, right?

I call her to double-check. So apparently you can't cook it frozen. Well, okay, so we're standing around a twelve-pound frozen turkey and we have five hours until Shabbat starts, minus four hours for cooking…

Maybe we should blow on it.

Friday, late morning. My sister and I go back out to the shuk and return with an extra-large plastic blue basin, diameter of about 100 cm. (It ended up being a good investment; we now use it as a baby bathtub.) In the meantime, my husband turns on the *dud chashmal* (electric water heater) in preparation for the vast amounts of hot water this job is going to need.

We put the turkey in the basin and fill it up with hot water. After ten minutes, the water is ice-cold, so we dump and repeat. And again, and again – sorry, Kinneret. It's Thanksgiving; I'm sure you understand.

Once the turkey is thawed, we put it in the pan and stuff it with the amount of stuffing which fits inside a twelve-pound turkey (i.e. not as much as you'd think). The rest of the stuffing goes into a separate covered pan, and both pans go into the oven. This is not as simple as it sounds, since our young-married-couple giant toaster oven is roughly the same size as … well, as a twelve-pound turkey. It takes a little bit of maneuvering, is all I'm saying.

We're cutting it close. I don't know whether or not the amount of time left before Shabbat will give us the perfect turkey, and I don't want to mess with my mother's turkey-roasting directions (which includes a certain amount of "cook the turkey at this angle for this many minutes, rotate ninety degrees on this axis, cook, flip, cook, flip, cook"), and we all know how important it is to get the turkey right.

Friday night. Thanksgiving Shabbat dinner is a success. The turkey is perfect. The cranberry-apple kugel is great. The extra stuffing is delicious. If we were one of those families who go around the table saying what we're thankful for (we are *not*), I would be saying that I'm thankful that we were able to pull this thing off.

And then a hand-sized chunk of ceiling falls right into the stuffing.

So yeah, that was the last time I celebrated Thanksgiving in Israel.

Making Myself at Home

Eden Farber

Eden grew up in Atlanta, GA, and made aliyah in 2014 at the age of 17. She studied on Kibbutz Ein HaNatziv for a year and then drafted to the Israeli Air Force. She finishes her service in the summer of 2017 and is hoping to start studying in the fall.

If you carry around a file folder that contains all of your important paperwork – original copies of every document in existence that proves you are who you say you are – it is probably best not to run through sprinklers while holding it. Twice.

This is my aliyah story.

I'm going to begin at the end (which is really the present, because nothing has "ended" yet). I'm halfway through my second week living on a beautiful kibbutz up north, in an intensive fifteen hours a day study program – and I've spent almost no time here. Every new day has brought a new office meeting; some paper was missing, some signature was needed, some account had to be opened. Whether running through sprinklers so as not to miss the last bus or waiting two hours for it to come, I have been traveling across the country, but I haven't exactly been traveling for pleasure. Attempting to navigate the bureaucratic system and become a fully functioning citizen has taken me in many seemingly senseless circles.

The scariest part of this *balagan* was doing the entire thing alone. My parents were not there to drop me off and wish me luck; my friends didn't take me out for ice cream after a long stressful day. This was not due to their negligence, of course. I was conscious that this would be my reality – how could I not have been – when I made aliyah alone at age 17.

However, alone turns out to be an entirely incorrect term for my experiences.

During my two-week long mission to sign up for health insurance, after being sent from place to place in the city of Beit She'an, wishing there was someone I could trust who could help me do this ostensibly simple task, I asked the security guard outside the post office if he knew where I needed to go. He nodded along as I explained my problem in broken Hebrew, and then went into the office, took my number, and went to the front desk to talk to the woman for me. Then he wrote out the steps of where exactly I needed to go and what the hours were.

A day or two later, in the same city, I asked a clerk outside how to get to the bus stop to Afula. Overhearing me from the sidewalk, a woman pushing her children in a double stroller, with groceries hanging off the handles, said: "I'll take you." Without a second glance, she walked me to my bus stop, and then turned around to go back and continue her errands. On our way, I heard someone shout out to me – the security guard from the day before had recognized me and wanted to know how I was doing. As difficult as it was for my pride to accept all these acts of kindness at once, I felt overwhelming appreciation for these people and their small but significant investments in me.

I'm proud to report, though, that these interactions were not rarities. Throughout my time here, every person – from government officials to taxi drivers to kibbutz neighbors to teachers and mentors – has treated me patiently and welcomingly. Every Israeli who heard that I had just moved here responded with a genuine, warm smile, and in my first few days my phone was flooded with calls and messages from distant family and old friends welcoming me to their homes and into their lives. I was overwhelmed with the feeling of belonging – not of the more traditional sense of belonging through speaking the language and knowing the culture, though. Rather, it was like walking into a person's home that you've never met before, being told to take off your shoes and given a hot drink, and hearing the simple but significant phrase, "Make yourself at home."

Fade back to my life in America. As proud as everyone around me was that I was "moving forward," and "making aliyah," (fulfilling a mitzvah and a Zionistic concept) the praise was always peppered with a certain kind of doubt or suspicion. I was not taking the usual path – finishing high school, going to college, working towards a substantial career, etc. – instead, I was following the dreams that I've carried since I was nine years old. The path less travelled was always less travelled for a reason. I would be lying if I said it was easy, that I never questioned myself, that I fit into the culture easily, that I never doubted my right to be here, or even that I never looked back; but I would also be lying if I said that with all of that, it wasn't absolutely worth it to be here.

From the moment I stepped off the plane and suddenly had to jump through bureaucratic hoops to get around, I realized that as challenging as it is to move to a foreign country, the culture of unconditional hospitality was a thing with which I had never truly interacted. And I loved it.

My aliyah story is not one of a Jew finding her home in Israel easily and simply, nor is it the story of a hero and soldier-to-be who followed her dreams without ever doubting herself. It's not the story of a perfect Jewish state or of a perfect Zionist dream come true. It's a story of trials and tribulations, overwhelming feelings of both comfort and loneliness – and the power of being in a culture that values caring about others as if they were family, both in ideology and in practice. It's the story of a person following their gut to do what they know they must. It's a story of strangers being overwhelmingly kind to strangers, not simply because we're all one big Jewish family, but because a society that preaches valuing others acts on it. It's a story of growing up and making tough decisions – and while aliyah is often treated as the universally correct one, I think it's important to acknowledge that every big decision and step in one's ideological identity should be valued and honored as much as the next one.

I will share with you one last tale: I was buying adapters to plug in my laptop, and trying to explain to the shopkeeper that I wanted America-to-Israel, not vice versa. "Why do you need that?" he asked impatiently in Hebrew. "I just moved here from America, and I don't have any," I responded likewise. Suddenly, his eyes lit up. "You moved here? Alone? Wow!" He continued to help me find everything I needed, and as I continued to speak to him in Hebrew, he tried to use as much English as he could muster up. He patiently helped me find the right money to pay with and, as I was leaving, he looked me in the eyes, smiled, and said in his thick Israeli accent, "Have a good luck, lady."

Elevator Speech

Sheila is a retired drama teacher and theater director. Her dream was to come to Israel to work on an archaeological dig, but she found that Israel called to her for her deepest life change. She now lives in Karmiel, Israel, which she considers to be a challenge and a blessing. She is the mother of two sons and lovingly shares her writings online. Sheila made aliyah in 2013.

On October 8, 2013, 62 passengers (and one dog) boarded El Al Flight LY8 to Israel, not as tourists, but to make aliyah – "to move up" – to become permanent residents. The arrival was long anticipated, not only because of the two days of travel from Los Angeles to Tel Aviv, but also because I personally was one of 62 passengers (but not necessarily the dog) who had made the decision to come home to Israel through "*ḥok ha-shvūt* – חוק השבות" – thereby fulfilling the promise of the prophetic Law of Return. Arrival in Israel of new olim is an event joyfully celebrated by the country, one in which we are made to feel welcomed, wanted, and home.

During the excitement of meeting and greeting one another, there was one recurring question: "Where are you moving?" It was somewhat reminiscent of being a college freshman moving into the dorms and being asked, "What's your major?" With a big smile, I would reply, "Karmiel" and, without fail, over 40 times, there would be a pause, a tilt of the head, a look askance, and then a hesitant reply along the lines of "Oh . . . well . . . that's a really pretty area." I began to worry.

The questions continued during my first few weeks in Karmiel: "Why did you move to Israel?" and, more specifically, "Why did you choose Karmiel?" I tried to answer thoughtfully and honestly: "I retired from 35 years of teaching, and this was a great opportunity for me," or "I am exhausted; I came to Israel to rest," or "The folks with the Nefesh B'Nefesh Go North program advised me that as a single, middle-aged woman (God, I HATE that description) making aliyah on her own with her dog, Karmiel was my best option." There would inevitably be a pause, a tilt of the head, a look askance, and then a hesitant reply along the lines of "Oh . . . Nefesh B' Nefesh." I worried a little bit more.

Should the conversation continue, it became of predictable assurance that I would be asked, "Where did you used to live? I don't recognize your accent."

First of all, let's clear something up. I am NOT the one with the accent – but putting that aside, Israelis are *aghast* when I tell them "Southern California." Not only is there disbelief that someone would leave the United States . . . at my age . . . alone . . . with her dog . . . but I have come to learn that, in the Israeli point of view, California IS the Kingdom of all Kingdoms of America. There is nothing subtle or guarded in their responses – they all think I am *meshuga*. That's right – I needed to completely uproot my life and move 15,000 miles just to confirm what we already know – I am one crazy girl!

It was around week four that I accepted that I was going to be meeting people for many more months to come, and that the inquiries were not going to end. Feeling particularly dissatisfied with the inadequacy of my answers, I decided to give some deeper thought to the questions. Now that I am here, experiencing Israel from the inside, are the reasons I decided to leave California specifically for Karmiel, still the same? I went back to my freshman year Public Speaking 101 notes (yellowed though they may be) and considered preparing one of those Toastmasters recommended, hit a home run out of the park, 30-second "elevator speeches." Bright, witty, sincere, clear, void of controversy or criticism. A 30-second prepared answer that would leave the questioner feeling satisfied with the answer while eliminating my dread that this was "... another fine mess I'd (sic) gotten myself into, Stanley."

Some deep contemplation and lots more soul searching was needed.

Why did I come to Israel? Why did I choose Karmiel? Why did I leave California?

1. There are the many pragmatic reasons that motivated my decision to move – retirement, a socialized medicine program, and monthly financial support from the government, to state a few.

2. There are the romantic reasons – the adventure, the newness, the "I just want to see what it is like to live somewhere else," the deeply buried "maybe I will meet a swarthy Israeli diplomat who will find me exotic and enchanting" fantasies that filled me with apprehensive excitement.

3. There are the "awareness of my mortality" reasons – my nervous breakdown, bad DNA from a mom who had breast cancer and a dad with a bad heart, the loss of a dear friend whose car got hit by a flying sheet of metal while driving down the freeway, which killed him instantly, the realization that I don't want to be sitting at Denny's one night with friends pondering, "I wonder what it would have been like," or "I wish I would have ..." I do not want to have any items left on my bucket list as the end draws near.

4. And finally, maybe it's time to accept that I truly *am* one "crazy son-of-a-bitch-loony hen" who, at best, will stand in front of a mirror shouting, "I tried, God dammit – at least I did that!"

But all of this is far too verbose for a 30-second elevator speech.

Why did I move to Israel and, in particular, to Karmiel – the north? Why did I leave California? The simple answer is "because I am a Jewish girl." But what does that mean? How deep does that go? My family was not observant Jews when we lived in Orange County in the 60s. We were far more Jewish in the eyes of the John Birch Society than we ever were in religious practice. And the closest I ever got to being a Zionist (not even sure what the word meant back then) was putting pennies, nickels, and dimes in the JNF *pushke*. The money was used to plant forests in Israel.

When I would bring my half-filled blue and white tin can to Sunday school, I would envision Moses and the wandering Jews swinging in hammocks from the trees I planted. And when I came on my pilot trip last February, I wanted to find "my trees," certain that the once small saplings planted by The Jewish National Fund over 50 years ago had grown taller and stronger than I was, and that I could be led to the forest and shown the "Thanks Little Sheila" plaque. I was that naïve.

It is said that if you want to find the strength of Israel, you go to Jerusalem, for the Holy City is the father to us all. But if you want to find the heart of Israel, you go north to the gentler and more soothing Galilee. She is the mother. Karmiel is in the lower Galilee, and it is beautiful here; gentle and soothing. I wake up each day to the most gorgeous blue skies framing the beautiful mountains to the north. Thirty-five miles to the east is the Sea of

Galilee and Tiberius, places profoundly meaningful in ancient Israel. Whether you are Jewish or a follower of Jesus, you cannot help but be moved by these locations of historical and spiritual significance. To the west is the Mediterranean Sea, the cities of Akko and Haifa, simultaneously ancient and modern – ports that have protected Israel from harm yet occasionally served as the gateways to invasion.

I am the only English speaker in my apartment building. Most of the residents are from Russia or Ukraine. A couple are from Ethiopia. Another handful are from Argentina or Uruguay. I hear Russian, Spanish, Tigrinya, and Yiddish. They are all warm and welcoming, offering to help me in whatever broken English they have. There are many children who live in my neighborhood. I see them go off to school each morning – walking hand in hand, laughing, skipping. Most want to stop and pet Molly Sylvester, my beloved dog. They love her already. I wander up the Galil where I purchase goods from Russians and Arabs. The people of Israel are all immigrants from somewhere in the world. I cannot tell you what an Israeli looks like, for this city is a tremendous melting pot of people who, for the most part, came to Israel through exile. A few of us came by choice.

But here is the thing – regardless of their country of birth, everyone speaks Hebrew. There is a mezuzah on every door. There is understanding, acceptance, and laughter despite the challenges inherent in adjusting from the life people knew in Russia, Ukraine, Argentina, Ethiopia, Uruguay, or maybe even America. I wonder if this is what America once felt like to the Polish, Irish, Italian, and German immigrants at end of the 19th century, and what the Hispanic, Vietnamese, Korean and Persian immigrants were seeking one hundred years later.

As I start to look at Israel from the inside, this land of so much conflict and strife, this land of milk and honey, I see people coming together to create good lives for themselves and their families and also something that is much bigger – the drive to ensure the survival of Israel and the future of their children/grandchildren/great-grandchildren. I see a country willing to help us financially, to send us to school, to teach us the language, to provide us with excellent, free medical care, to give us citizenship, and to welcome us home.

So yes, I have come up with my elevator speech. And it is not even 30 seconds. It is only one word.

Why did I come to Israel, specifically Karmiel? Why did I leave California?

To paraphrase Tevye, "That, I can tell you in one word – HOPE."

Now, all I have to do is find an elevator!

How I Became an Aliyah Snob

Uri Pilichowski

Rabbi Uri Pilichowski is a Rebbe at Yeshivat Migdal Hatorah in Modi'in, Israel. He also teaches Israel political advocacy to students in America and Israel. Before making aliyah, Rabbi Pilichowski was a rabbi in Beverly Hills, CA and Boca Raton, FL. His wife, Aliza, and their six children all live in "The Pilichowski Palace" in Mitzpe Yericho, where they frequently host tourist and student groups and discuss the imperative for Jews to live in Yehuda and Shomron. Uri made aliyah in 2014.

The first time I heard the phrase, it took me by surprise; especially considering its source. My friend, a fellow colleague in the rabbinate, was expressing his annoyance about a Facebook comment pushing him and his community to move to Israel. "These aliyah snobs that just moved to Israel," he snorted. "They've been in the country less than a year, and all they do is preach aliyah."

I didn't really know what to make of his complaint. Did he have a problem with aliyah? He was a rabbi, could he really have an issue with people preaching? Was it the fact that they'd only recently made aliyah that irked him?

Although he didn't know it at the time of his comment, my wife, Aliza, and I had already decided to make aliyah within the next few months. I wondered if I would become an "aliyah snob." Most of all, I wondered what turned a person into an "aliyah snob."

I have never been happier in my life. My prayers to live in *Eretz Yisrael* were literally answered. For a decade, I'd dreamed that I'd be able to live in *Eretz Yisrael*. I'd prayed for it, wished for it, and imagined it. Today, I live it. I am living my and countless others' dream. I live with the excitement of destiny fulfilled, and dreams realized. It is absolutely amazing.

My family and I moved here a little over 160 days ago (yes, we, or at least I, count each day). We live in an amazing community, Mitzpe Yericho, with people who respect each other, help each other, and share our values. I have neighbors who seem to help us in a new way every day. My family and I live in a beautiful large home that we could never have afforded in America. It has a view that overlooks the Judean Desert, Jericho, the Jordanian Mountains, and on the walk to my synagogue, the Dead Sea. My children attend a public school that rivals any observant day school in America (forget about the tuition difference – I pay 500 shekels a month for three children). My kids are learning Hebrew better than Jewish high school seniors and have transitioned seamlessly into a new school with new friends.

I understand that not everyone shares my experiences. I know that aliyah is tougher for some than others. I moved to Israel once before, and after eight years, moved back to America for ten years, only to return this year. I know of the financial, emotional, and physical struggles families suffer when coming to Israel. Yet, with all the challenges moving to Israel can incur, I know one thing that makes it worth it.

While in America, we aimed to strengthen our Jewish identity. We created programming, curricula and events to ensure the continuity of Jewish life, culture, and tradition. We extolled our connection to Israel, taught Zionism and Israel advocacy. Yet we were on the sidelines of the Jewish future.

It would be naive to think that the future of the Jewish people is anywhere but in Israel. Whether you're religious, secular, or somewhere in between, you have to acknowledge that leading Jewish thought, tradition, and culture is all taking place in Israel. In Israel, we aren't strengthening our identity, we are creating it. The excitement in the streets of Israel, the constant building, growth, and development is palpable. We've all felt it on visits, missions, and vacations here. There is a sense of pride, of shared enthusiasm, of a partnership in something much larger than ourselves that is happening all around us.

When I pray at the Kotel and look up at the Temple Mount, I know that our future has arrived. In my settlement, when I look out over my porch at the western bank of the Jordan River, something my grandfather could only have dreamed of while he lay in a barracks in Auschwitz, I know our future has arrived. When F-16s fly by my porch and dip their wings, so close that I can see the Star of David on their tail, I know our future has arrived. Most of all, when I see hundreds of Jewish children skipping through the streets of Jerusalem's Old City on their way to study their first words of Torah, I know that our people's future is here in Israel. New immigrants to Israel don't want to be on the sidelines for our people's future, we want to play a part in it.

People ask me if I ever see my excitement of living in Israel dying down. I know in my first month here I couldn't sleep through the night, I was so overjoyed to be here. I sleep fine now, exhausted by a day's work. Yet, as I watch the sunrise each morning over the Jordanian mountains, it's hard for me to believe I'll ever get used to living in Israel.

Do all of these feelings and emotions make me a snob? Does boasting to my friends of my commute through the very paths our ancestors walked make me an "aliyah snob?" I don't know, and frankly, I don't care. Maimonides wrote that one who truly loves something – he was talking about the love of God – can't stop talking about it. He wrote that love of God was the driving force that pushed Avraham to tell everyone and anyone, even at the risk of his life, about God. I think fresh olim, new immigrants to Israel, are so excited about creating our future, of being a part of something so much larger than themselves, and of setting Jewish destiny, that they can't stop talking about it. If that makes us "aliyah snobs," then so be it. I'll take it as a compliment.

Seven Months an Israeli

Talya Woolf

Talya is a litigator and young-at-heart artist wandering around Israel with her Nikon camera. She is an imma of two wonderful boys, the author of several blogs, and wife to a handsome web developer. She loves traveling, cooking, art-ifying anything that moves, sampling fine wines, and meeting new people. Her calligraphy and lettering work, as well as her photography, can be found at amiraphoto.com. Her blogs can be read on The Times of Israel as well as at forloveoftheusa.blogspot.com. Talya made aliyah in 2015.

I have been living the Israeli dream for seven months now, and it still occasionally feels like I'm on vacation. I worked for three months in the South Tel Aviv area until I gave birth, joined an art *chug* in my community, met new people, and made new friends. I visited cousins, dealt with bureaucracy (and the damned post office), rode the bus daily, and settled into life in this country halfway around the globe.

At about three months in, I learned a vital lesson and it hasn't changed since. Life in Israel is about the bigger picture. It isn't about the daily grind – it's about the weekly one, the monthly one, and soon enough, the yearly one.

We can so easily get caught up in the frustrations of dealing with doctors and the medical system, the buses and their infernal everything (schedules, drivers, passengers), the damned post office, inconsiderate Israelis, the random terrorist attack –

I know I have. There were days when I was in tears from the anger I felt at the fact that THIS COUNTRY was so backwards. There were weeks where I wondered how THIS COUNTRY, so forward-thinking and tech savvy, couldn't figure out its bureaucratic crap. How THIS COUNTRY could have such a horrendous public transportation system when it got to start from scratch, and how THIS COUNTRY could be so unbelievably third-world.

And then one day, I got on the bus (either the 68 or the 70) and experienced another ridiculous "bus event," as I've started calling them. I believe it was the time we took a tight turn and – yes, it finally happened – *we hit a car*. I was sitting in the front and heard the crunch. I had been headed home in the hopes of getting to hug my toddler before bedtime. And then this.

I thought briefly about getting upset, and then… I didn't. I realized I was amused. Just another ridiculous bus story, just another experience… but in the larger scheme of things, I was fine, the bus was fine, no one was injured. Just the car's side mirror and part of the bumper were. A bus ticket-checker came onto the bus and started making fun of the driver to me in rapid Hebrew. When I asked him to slow down since I was a new olah, he guessed, "Espanol?" to which I responded, "*Anglit.*" He walked away; I don't know why. But instead of being offended, I was tickled because he thought I was from Spain.

Eventually, the driver got back on the bus and we proceeded home, but my attitude had shifted.

This country is a baby, (at the time of writing this) only 67 years old. My father is older than this country. She started with nothing. Not much infrastructure, only 806,000 people, and a war that demolished large chunks of cities.

She now has over 8 million people living within her borders, an 865% growth in less than seven decades, and she's had to grow and expand, quickly, to accommodate everyone. I think THIS COUNTRY should be given a break.

Each day here is a new adventure. Each day holds the possibility of being aggravated by red tape, too-hot weather, idiot bus drivers, rude Israelis, you name it. But I've also experienced the good in the midst of those days of tears. Passengers yelling at drivers to let someone on (or off), strangers helping older people by pushing or lifting their bubbe carts, Arab strangers showing cartoons to your toddler on their phone, store owners (strangers) staying open for you and giving you the items you need, simply trusting you to come back to pay, random neighbors (strangers) lending you maternity clothing, strangers walking next to you on the street, wishing you a healthy and easy birth. Strangers living in this country, Jewish and Arab alike, doing things to help other strangers.

I can't say exactly what triggered the change. Maybe I finally found humor in the futility of having patience for certain things here ... maybe the #onlyinIsrael situations finally tipped the scales, maybe I simply got used to the differences between my two countries and let go of certain unrealistic expectations, maybe my pregnancy hormones calmed down that day, maybe my quirky sense of humor finally returned – maybe all of the above.

All I know is that there are bound to be situations where I want to pull my hair out and cry (damned post office). And while I am sure this happens in all countries, I likely expect more from Israel because she is mine, like we do from our own family. Israel is a family (of strangers). Some of us are great, some misunderstood, some annoying, some are clueless, but most of us do the best we can for each other.

So I smile, laugh, or roll my eyes at whatever inane thing happened today, and tell myself something a very wise and intentionally happy man taught me when he made aliyah:

It's another beautiful day in Paradise.

Becoming Bilingual (Or at Least Trying!)

How Do I Get To ...?

Susan Leibtag

Susan made aliyah with her husband Bernard in January 2012. She has two daughters who made aliyah with their families in 2008, and a son living in Chicago with his family. Susan works virtually for the Johns Hopkins University Bloomberg School of Public Health, as a librarian and quality control specialist. She lives in Modi'in.

See, now that is a question I am always asking other people, or, actually, I am always asking Waze.

Before I go anywhere new, I not only put the location in Waze, but I look at it on Google Maps, just to see the route beforehand, look at the "street view" so I know what to look for when I get there, and consider alternate routes. I mean, I investigate thoroughly.

That is because I am MORTALLY TERRIFIED of being in the wrong location – um, with good reason.

Israel is not a country in which you have "fun" being lost. It's not an adventure, it's just plain scary.

So here I was, driving along minding my own business, and there's a young woman who is stopped in the middle of the street in my neighborhood. While everyone else was honking and gesticulating around her for delaying their arrival at their destination for all of 20 seconds, I looked at her and she waved at me desperately.

So I pulled over, and she asked me where a certain street was. In Hebrew. She was Israeli.

Hahahaha! SHE asked ME! And she expected me to explain! In Hebrew! Hahahaha!

So I knew exactly where she wanted to go, but when I started explaining, after the (Hebrew) expression, "First, turn around," my words did that same funny trick they always do – they start doing acrobatics as they are about to come out of my mouth.

I literally could not speak. So I decided, well, that's not HER fault, and said, in English, "Follow me." She looked at me in shock, "*Yesh lach zman*?" (You have time?). And instead of answering that taking ten minutes to show her is less embarrassing than trying to explain it with my acrobatic Hebrew, I nodded.

At one point, after about five minutes of driving, I gesticulated for her to pull up next to me and I asked her which direction on this road she was looking for. Then I explained IN HEBREW what she should do. She was very grateful and drove on.

On my way home, I repeated what I'd said to her about 100 times – was it correct? Did I tell her to turn left when I should have told her to turn right?

What if she ends up in Ramallah??? What did I do???

I will never know if she found the place.

My only consolation is that if you try to enter Ramallah, the army stops you, and maybe a soldier will tell her how to get where she was going.

I should have just told her how to install Waze on her phone.

I Have No Idea What You Just Said

Susan Leibtag

These three things happened to me just today:

PHONE CALL #1:

Got a phone call. Someone speaking Hebrew reallyreallyquickly. I answered, *"Lo hevanti"* (transl: HUH?)

She spoke a bit more slowly – something about my husband and *challot*. Hmm, knowing my husband, who is still recovering from the trauma that was Tax Season 2015, he probably bought *challot* and left them in the store.

OK, I answered (in Hebrew that is "OK"), he'll come back for them. Since there was not the usual moment of silence after I speak Hebrew (during which the Israelis realize that I have not understood a word of the conversation), I figured I'd gotten it right.

RESTAURANT:

We have been here for three years. We have learned a lot of Hebrew, okay? Really! So when I walked into the restaurant today, and they asked me if I wanted the English menu, I declined the offer. I mean, really, dude.

Waiter comes to take our order. We know what we are doing, do not mess with us. He asks us all of the usual questions, and we answer like pros. We got this.

Then he said something else. It was a question. Clearly he wanted me to choose between one thing and another. I caught a word, and repeated it. I glanced at my husband, who looked likewise clueless. The waiter repeated the word followed by a questioning tone. I gave my all-time favorite answer, *"B'seder."* I was hoping he didn't ask if I'd like a touch of cyanide in my omelet, or if I preferred that he serve me bread from two days ago.

Seriously, I have no idea what he asked me.

The meal was fine, though, and I didn't taste whatever it was I chose to add. Or not add.

Close call.

PHONE CALL #2:

Then I got a call from the Hyundai dealership. I mean, I think it was the Hyundai dealership. We don't own a Hyundai, but we used to. *"Susan?"* the nice lady asked. *"Ken,"* I answered. (I got this).

Then about forty thousand Hebrew words came out of her mouth. I got none of them. What I ASSUMED was that there was some kind of sale going on and it was incumbent upon me to take advantage of it.

I took a risk. I said, IN HEBREW, "I am not interested in a new car right now, but thank you." Apparently, I did not say something entirely stupid. In other words, it really was a lady from Hyundai and there really was a sale.

She proceeded to talk more. Many, many words of Hebrew. Finally, I had to shut her up, I mean it was such a waste of her time. I said, "Well, thank you and Shabbat Shalom!"

So, all in all, not bad for someone who is totally clueless. I can fake it pretty well after three years. And there's always *"B'seder"* and *"Lo hevanti."*

I Have No Idea What You Just Said, Pt. 2

Susan Leibtag

So, Hebrew continues to be my greatest struggle here, although I have had people tell me my Hebrew is pretty good. I mean, I can navigate important websites like online supermarkets, the bank, and the *Kupat Cholim*, and it's all good when I work on the emails for my shul, which have to be in English and Hebrew.

But it's the conversations that do me in. I. Can. Not. Speak. Hebrew. To. An. Israeli.

Take, for instance, the past few days:

1. LESS HUMILIATING:

We went to talk to a car dealer. In Israel, car buying is actually pretty easy, because there is no haggling (surprised, aren't you?). Seriously, the price is the price. And the inventory is low (I mean, it's a small country, where would they store the cars, after all?), so you get what you can get, and don't worry about this trim package and that trim package, etc. etc. At least, that is our experience.

The car salesman did not speak English. His Hebrew was pretty clear, though. But here I am, listening to him and wondering how much of what I THINK he said, he actually said. And how much I got wrong. I usually end up asking this question: "What is it that I HAVE TO DO RIGHT NOW?" – that usually gets me a clear answer.

2. A BIT MORE HUMILIATING:

Went today to get our old car inspected before it is sold. Inspector guy comes to get me and we sit down, and he goes over the details of the inspection certificate. I have no idea what he is saying, so I keep asking, "But is it OK to sell right now?" I don't know what he said in response to that. It could have been yes, it could have been no, it could have been maybe.

Then the inspector guy keeps talking, and he TEARS UP THE INSPECTION CERTIFICATE. I'm totally horrified – oh my gosh, what did I just agree to??? I say, now what should I do, thinking I've just authorized him to make thousands of shekels in repairs without realizing it. I figured he's going to say, "Well, sit yourself down, honey, 'cause we are going to do thousands of shekels in repairs on your car! Hahahaha!!!! Sucka!"

Instead, he says, "Well, what do you WANT to do?" By this time, I'm getting a headache. I say, "I want to go." He says, "So go." I still have no idea what happened, but I walked out with a new certificate (at least, that's what I think it is).

3. EXTREMELY HUMILIATING:

While I'm waiting for the car to be inspected, I get a call from the mailman. Yes, the mailman himself. He has a package for me, and wants to come between... and, for the life of me, I think he is saying between "1:30 and 1:00." I'm pretty sure I got that wrong, so I say, "Well, I'm not home now." He hesitated, probably thinking, "What the heck do I care if she's home now or not?"

He said, again, "I'll come between..." and again I'm sure it was between 1:30 and 1:00. I give up and say OK. The worst that can happen is that I won't be home and he'll leave a note. I get off the phone, and all of the other people in the waiting room are kinda looking at me (maybe that was my imagination). And slowly I realize that the time he gave me was between 11 and 1, not 1:30 and 1:00. When he said *"achad esrei"* I kept thinking *"achad v'chetzi."*

BTW, the package was delivered. I think the mailman was snickering when he dropped it off.

The Loneliness of Not Knowing

Celeste Aronoff

Celeste was on her way to rabbinical school in Los Angeles when she took a slight detour to Israel and unexpectedly fell in love with the country. Her love affair led to three years of working to combine her lifetime dedication to spiritual practice with the Torah she's passionate about. She shares her thoughts on her blog, www.thelazyradical.blogspot.com. She was born in Brooklyn, grew up mostly in Kansas City, and lived in Jerusalem. Celeste made aliyah in 2015, though has returned to the U.S. for the time being.

The hardest part about making aliyah so far (and I know it can get a lot harder) is that I'm used to being a really, really competent adult. And suddenly, I'm not. The entire cultural competency I've amassed, all the nuances and subtleties that I've learned to navigate in my personal and professional life, are mostly moot. And it's evident the minute I open my mouth.

It's not that I can't speak Hebrew. I can make it through most conversations pretty adequately. But as a communications person by education and profession, language has always been my best tool. When I speak Hebrew, my giant box of metaphorical tools is reduced to the equivalent of a hammer, a screwdriver, and a few misshapen nails. When I speak English, I can access every tool there is with finesse and grace and eloquence, constructing and creating ideas that influence the world around me.

I can express sophisticated, complex, nuanced thoughts with lyrical poetry and compelling prose.

In Hebrew, I'm lucky if I can find the store I'm looking for, get accurate directions (as accurate as any Israeli ever provides), and ask for a menu in English so I at least have a chance of ordering the meal I intended. My fumbling with Hebrew, and the incredibly kind reassurance others give me that I will get better, is sometimes the most meaningful interaction I have in this new language. I have been overwhelmed at the unexpected kindness of Israelis, Jewish and Christian and Arab and Circassian, who offer me the right word, who themselves stumble in English to compensate for my lack, and who tell me not to worry, that I will learn *le'at, le'at*, slowly, slowly. I would be happier learning slowly if they didn't speak so quickly!

In Hebrew, even though I feel a mystical connection to thousands of years of history, religion, and identity, I am isolated from the ordinary conversations around me. I'm used to being able to read receipts, signs, bills, notices, newspapers, flyers, blackboards and white boards, bus and train schedules, web pages, nutritional labels, grocery aisle signs, ads, billboards, prescriptions, the sides of trucks and buses, food labels, magazine covers, recipes, synagogue bulletins, Facebook posts, Google results, and on and on. I'm used to being able to read and understand all the little clues in my environment that center me in my world.

Even with all the Hebrew I've learned in university, in ulpan, and in life, I walk through the streets of Jerusalem sounding out words phonetically like a first-grader. And then, it's just a guess if I've got the right vocalization or meaning. When a friend tells me that a sign on the back of a truck is a play on words, I miss the playfulness entirely. I don't get the joke when it's in Hebrew.

In English, I get the joke before it's even told because I am fluent the way we are when we share not just the technology of a language, but the culture and feeling and meaning contained in it. I get the text and the subtext and the subtleties and all the nuances that weave connections between the teller and the listener, joining us in a shared understanding that ends with a laugh between us. And nothing makes you feel more like you belong than getting the joke.

The loneliness I feel here in Israel – it isn't a lack of company or friends or even familiarity; I love the adventure of exploring and discovering this amazing place. But the loneliness I feel every day is the loneliness of not being able to connect through words, to confidently have the most ordinary exchanges with total strangers. These ordinary conversations connect us with life in the smallest and loveliest ways all the time – with the bus driver or grocery store clerk or bank teller or bookseller. I can take a few clumsy steps towards them, but then I reach my own limits, my own inability to keep up with the conversation, to follow their lead, to complete the linguistic transaction.

I'm relieved to be learning Hebrew, though. At least Hebrew makes a kind of sense, with its *shorashim* (roots) that expand and contract in endless conjugations, connected nouns and verbs with shared meaning. Better for sure than to be one of those brave souls learning English, with its incomprehensible mix of linguistic influences offering nothing as eloquent as *shorashim* dancing with prefixes and suffixes in an ancient rhythm.

I am grateful to all those who have been so kind and patient, for all those who correct me and offer to teach me more, and all those who have welcomed me so warmly to a country I'm not very good at yet. And I'm looking forward to the day when I'll be the one with the expertise in this holy language, able to bestow patience and graciousness myself.

On Playing Chicken, Speaking Hebrew, and Emergency Haircuts

Tzippy Levy

For an immigrant, one of the best things about living in Jerusalem is that you don't need to choose between English and Hebrew. There's plenty of opportunity to speak in English, without it being a bubble like some nearby towns, whose names I won't mention but rhyme with Skefrat. The city has a wide variety of people who speak no English, people who speak some English, people who speak excellent English, and people who speak English as a mother tongue. My preference is to speak Hebrew to people whose native language is not English (unless they're more comfortable in English) and English to people whose native language is English.

Easier said than done, especially when I run into English speakers who have that same tendency. You know, that awkward moment when you're speaking Hebrew to a fellow English speaker and neither of you wants to be the first one to switch?

I mean, you're an English speaker, they're an English speaker, and you both know it. But you don't want to say it straight out. So maybe you try to exaggerate your accent a little bit. Or you let a common English phrase slip into the conversation, hoping the other person will note your lack of Israeli accent. Or, if you're on the telephone, maybe you'll tell your daughter out of the side of your mouth, in English, to *please* stop cutting her hair with the scissors from her sister's pencil case already, because there are only so many miracles you can work. For example.

But, whatever happens, you *don't blink first*. Because maybe you're wrong. Maybe you're just imagining that accent (you were always kind of weak with accents, anyway). Or maybe they grew up in Israel, and they have a slight accent because their parents are English speakers, but they really prefer Hebrew. Or maybe they're an English speaker, but they're trying to improve their Hebrew by speaking it all the time, and if you switch to English, they'll be offended.

And that would be the worst. You don't want to give offense. Because you know how it feels. We all know the shame of talking to an Israeli in what we thought was perfectly decent Hebrew, and then they answer you in broken English. The sinking feeling of *"Oh no I'm a fraud, they can all see right through me. What gave me away? Did I speak too slowly? Was my accent too strong? Did I accidentally say "Are you using the bathroom" instead of "Are you free?"*

As if our attempts at mastering the language were all for naught, as if speaking to us in Hebrew is just so horribly painful that this person would rather tough it out in a language he barely speaks than listen to our nails-across-a-chalkboard Hebrew.

Yes, I know that this is an overreaction. But being a non-native speaker of the local language really has a way of bringing out the self-consciousness in a person.

The most common example of this phenomenon comes when giving or asking for directions. Because you are a total stranger whom they stop in the middle of the street, they don't know whether you speak English or not. So they ask you for directions in Hebrew, and you don't want to insult them by responding in English (except for the fact that I've been here nine years and I still don't know how to say "block" in Hebrew – as in, "Go three blocks and make a right" – but I digress. As usual. Am I in the middle of a parenthetical statement here? What's going on? Close parentheses). Okay, that's better. Where was I?

Ahh. You give them directions in English-accented Hebrew, they say "*Toda*" in English-accented Hebrew, and then they go on their way and hopefully don't get lost, especially if they're in a car, because you don't have a car and you don't always know whether certain streets go one or two ways. Sorry about those driving tickets.

These directions-giving conversations happen all the time, but they're also not as bad, because they only last for ten seconds and you may never see that person again – or, at least, if you do see them again, they probably won't remember you.

It's a little more complicated when it's someone you speak to on a regular basis, like a neighbor, co-worker, or fellow parent at your kid's school. These things can go on for years. Once you've already established someone as a Hebrew contact, it's hard to break the habit. Usually, it doesn't get that far, though – one of you will cave early on and say, "You're an English speaker, right?" (As if there are two possible answers to that question, with that accent). But if you get through three conversations in Hebrew, that means you have what's called in halachic terms a "*chazaka*," and you're never allowed to speak English to that person. Which is fine, because odds are that they speak Hebrew over English out of ideological reasons, anyway.

You know, the only thing more awkward than the situation above would be if an English speaker who currently speaks with me in Hebrew were to read this and then all of a sudden start talking to me in English the next time they see me. I'm cringing just imagining that, and I can't even explain why.

Okay, so nobody do that. If you currently speak to me in Hebrew, continue speaking to me in Hebrew. For that matter, if you currently speak to me in English, let's switch to Hebrew. It is, after all, the Holy Tongue. And if you want directions from me, *definitely* ask me in Hebrew.

(But if you're in a car, maybe check the traffic signs before actually following my instructions.)

Does this Ever Happen to You ... ?

Gila Leibtag-Rose

> Gila lives in Modi'in. She has five children and lots of times
> even knows where they all are. She is a copywriter/editor in
> her free time. Otherwise, she spends her days drinking coffee,
> conjugating Hebrew badly, wondering why numbers have to
> have a gender, and actively practicing subpar parenting. Gila
> made aliyah in 2008.

So you're talking to someone in Hebrew, and you're catching
most of the conversation, which you feel pretty good about.
[Insert pat on back here.] Then, suddenly, theybegintalking
veryveryfast. And you are quickly losing track of the conversation. "...something...something...bathroom...something...
something... batteries... something... something... vaccina-
tion..." "Huh?" you start asking yourself, feeling your hold on
things quickly and decisively slipping. You nod, throw in the
occasional grunt, but this is way out of your league. Did she
just say "fettucine"??

Suddenly, the conversation comes to a screeching halt. And
she's looking at you expectantly. Oh god, you realize, with a
fear akin to seeing a great white swimming right for you, she's
waiting for a *reaction*. She wants you to *say* something! And
you, of course, lost the thread of this conversation someplace in
between "tablecloths" and "Netanyahu." (At least, that's what it

sounded like.) Is she expecting a hearty guffaw? An expression of outrage? A murmur of sympathy? You have no clue whether her dog just died, her husband was promoted, or she's against the conversion bill. Or maybe for it?

Readers, loyal and otherwise! Never be stuck in this quandary again! Learn the patented "Aliyah By Accident" (that's my personal online blog) vague response, appropriate for all situations and scenarios! It works like this:

1. Smile slightly, in a way which can be construed as sympathetic or agreeable (and really those are your only two choices, because let's face it, even if she just expressed admiration for Cruella de Vil, or announced her intention to come to work wearing only undies, are you really in a position to debate this? We thought not.)
2. Raise your eyebrows just a touch, to vaguely indicate surprise.
3. Mumble, "Ha-ha … mmmm … ahem … ahem."

Trust me, after two years, I can assure you this works. Contact me if you would like private lessons.

Numbers

Gila Leibtag-Rose

Today, I reached a big milestone in my absorption. I said the number 7,500 in Hebrew. And I think I even got it right.

Every oleh has absorption goals. Some people want to "Drink Turkish coffee out of those tiny, tiny cups" or "Blithely wear t-shirts with inappropriate sayings because you don't realize they're inappropriate" or "Serve dinner to children at 8 p.m. (instead of getting ready to herd them into bed at that time so you can collapse on the couch, I mean clean up)."

For this year, I chose the lofty goal of "Writing checks in Hebrew." Until now, I took the easy way out and just wrote all my checks in English, because anything with four digits or more stumped me. But, I told myself, you are Israeli now. You must do as the Israelis do: Go to Eilat for Hanukkah.

No, no, not THAT. We're talking about numbers. Pay attention, please!

Right. So I decided that this year, I would work on my Israeliness through numbers. Unfortunately, my go-to pal Google Translate is of no use here. Type in "1,465" in English, and it helpfully spits back, "1,465" in Hebrew.

But I will do it. And, in fact, at the bank today, I did NOT need to say, "*Elef PLOOSE elef PLOOSE elef PLOOSE elef PLOOSE elef PLOOSE elef PLOOSE elef. V'od chamesh mayot.*"

Yay me!

Next on the list:

Answering the phone with, "*Ahh-lan!*"

Be All You Can Be

Jen Maidenberg

Most of us spend our entire lives figuring out who we are.

Parallel to this, we also seek the confidence to *admit* to ourselves who we are and *share* that self with others.

It can be an entire life's work.

Imagine, then, being reborn smack dab in the middle of that project.

This is what it has been for me to make aliyah.

Some will say just the opposite.

That making aliyah was like "coming home."

That moving to Israel allowed them to finally "find themselves;" to finally feel a part *of* something, rather than apart *from*.

And there are elements of that sentiment I can relate to, but I wouldn't say this has been my overarching experience until now.

Moving to Israel was a move away from who I am.

I am a communicator.

This is what I do. It's what I love to do and it's what I'm good at.

I'm also a relationship builder and an information gatherer.

And those are probably the three hardest things to do and be when you are a new immigrant, especially one in a country in which the main language is not your native tongue.

So why did I move to Israel?

For lots of reasons.

Good ones.

Reasons I stand by and do not regret.

But just as we do after many of the big life decisions we make – getting married, having kids, taking a new job – I ask myself now:

Who am I?

Who am I now?

Am I still me?

Some of my family and friends would insist I managed to be "me" even here in Israel. That I found a way to be the communicator, the relationship builder, and the information gatherer despite the challenges of language and culture.

On some days, I'd agree (and pat myself on the back, thank you very much).

But then there are the unforgiving days...

The days when I run into another parent in the parking lot, and I take that breath.

You know that breath?

It's the one you hardly notice but you take it right before you jump into a casual conversation with a casual friend in the parking lot.

Before you just "shoot the shit."

You take that breath.

I take that breath.

But then I remember:

I'm not me anymore. Not exactly.

This me thinks, "It's going to be too, too hard for me to figure out which shit is the appropriate shit to shoot. And it'll be even harder for me to understand the shit she is shooting back to me in Hebrew."

And then I take another breath. This time, more of a sigh.

And I ask myself, "Is it worth the mild humiliation? Discomfort?"

I'm not sure.

So I don't.

This is never a question I asked myself before.

Never.

And, similarly, there are some days...

Days when I know it's really necessary for me to have a heart-to-heart with the teacher at my kid's school. And I force myself to have the conversation.

Not because I am "the communicator" or the "information gatherer," but because it's what I HAVE to do. It's on my to-do list. And maybe I have that conversation, but I know it's the mediocre version of what I could have pulled off in English.

And, oh how I judge myself afterwards.

And question myself.

In a way I never ever did before.

Never.

Because I knew who I was.

At least I thought I did...

Now, I'm not so sure.

Is who we are so fragile that POOF a move to a foreign country can change us?

Or do we just have to dig deeper, try harder to be all we are. In spite of ourselves...

I Didn't Recognize You With Your Pants On!

Akiva Gersh

Hebrew school. One might think it's a place where Jewish kids go to learn Hebrew. But those who have actually been through the Hebrew school system know the sad truth: You don't learn Hebrew in Hebrew school.

All those hours spent sitting in yet another classroom after yet another full day of public school just didn't quite constitute the right formula. Hebrew school utterly failed to motivate us to want to learn about Judaism or learn a new language we felt we would never use. Whether it was the fault of the students for not listening or caring enough, or the fault of the teachers for not knowing how to teach students who didn't listen or care enough, not much of anything was really learned, especially not any Hebrew. After eight years of Hebrew school, I remembered three words and three words alone: *abba, imma,* and *kelev.*

After a long spiritual journey led me back to my Jewish roots, I made aliyah in the summer of 2004. Though after learning in yeshiva for five years, I could successfully decipher a Talmudic debate (in Hebrew) about someone's ox goring someone else's worker, I, like many others before me, quickly realized that the Hebrew of the holy books wasn't going to help me order a coffee in the modern State of Israel.

But, fortunately, the early founders of the state were smart.

They came up with the ingenious ulpan system. Its very existence speaks volumes about the Jewish people's return to our homeland and, just as miraculous, the reestablishment of our ancient tongue. (We know that for 2,500 years, more than half of Jewish history, Hebrew was not the everyday language of the Jewish people. Even Herzl, the father of Zionism, didn't speak Hebrew!)

Like many others, I took advantage of free ulpan and dedicated five months of my life, five days a week, five hours a day to learning Modern Hebrew. And then I went back and did it again. It was quite a humbling experience, especially considering the fact that right before making aliyah I had completed my master's in Jewish education. The contrast was striking. My graduate degree did not prevent me from feeling like I was being flung back to first grade. I sat diligently at my desk trying to grasp the ins and outs of a language that, while so close to my soul, was so foreign to my lips. After 1000 hours of ulpan, I eventually gained enough confidence to start speaking Hebrew to real-life, Hebrew-speaking Israelis. But doing so opened up the gates to a whole world of embarrassing moments and funny mistakes every time I tried to ask a question, answer someone else's question or just basically say something about anything.

Possibly the only consolation was that I knew I wasn't alone. I knew that there was an entire community of other English-speaking olim who were also learning to speak Hebrew for the first time. Other people who, like me, could speak coherently and sometimes even eloquently in our native tongue about all kinds of complex issues and topics, but struggled in Hebrew to order a pizza with the right toppings, tell the person at the post office what we really needed, or understand all the amazing things our kids' teachers were saying about them.

In an attempt to avoid making mistakes, we rehearse our

lines in the car, while waiting in line at the store, and while on hold on the phone as if we are getting ready to get on stage for the performance of our lives. We write down what we want to say in advance and thank God every day for Google Translate. We try our hardest not to make mistakes in Hebrew in front of our kids, but we know, and they definitely know, that it inevitably happens. Sometimes, a lot.

But we learn to laugh. And get over it. And hope that the next time we have to open up our mouth it won't be as bad. And if it is, we laugh again.

In that spirit of learning to laugh at ourselves, I share the following list that I've compiled with the help of fellow olim. It offers a glimpse of some of those funny and even embarrassing moments we've experienced, we've witnessed and we've endured, all in the name of bringing ourselves back home and learning the language of the modern Israelites.

By the way, if you're an oleh and haven't made at least one of these mistakes (or something similar), you're lying.

Here we go:

A friend of mine was getting off the bus and told the bus driver that she had a suitcase *"b'tachtonim"* (in her underwear) rather than *"b'tachton"* (under the bus).

I am a doctor in a hospital, and I asked a nurse to give my patient *"ha'zona"* (the prostitute), instead of *"hazana"* (nutrition).

I once asked my patient to give me a deep breath, but instead of saying, *"Ten li neshima gedolah,"* I said, *"Ten li nishika gedolah!"* which means, "Give me big kiss."

I was asked how to get somewhere and instead of saying *"Lifnot ba'kikar,"* which means "Take a turn at the traffic circle," I said, *"L'hitpanot ba'kikar"* which means, "Urinate in the traffic circle."

In my husband's ulpan class was a huge guy, 6½ feet tall and likely weighing well over 300 pounds. He was traveling on a crowded bus, and when he reached his stop, the guy couldn't maneuver out of the bus in time. As the bus started up again, he shouted to the bus driver, *"Nahag nahag, rega! Rega! Ani tzarich laledet!"* ("I need to give birth!") instead of *"Ani tzarich la'redet"* ("I need to get off.") The entire bus took a look at the guy and burst out laughing.

When asked to speak about my relatives, I called them cabbage heads (*kruvim*) instead of family members (*krovim*).

My husband was asked to give a speech for his birthday party at work six months into aliyah. He talked with great pride about how he felt so happy about being a *"chatzil"* (eggplant) instead of saying *"chalutz"* (pioneer).

I was walking on the street and asked someone passing by, *"Mah ha'sha'ah* – do you know what time it is?" The man pointed to his naked wrist and said, *"Ain li musag* – I have no clue." I thought when he pointed to his wrist he was telling me he has no *"musag"*, meaning no wristwatch. Happy to use my newly learned word, I enthusiastically asked the next stranger who came along, *"Yesh l'cha musag* – Do you have a clue?" He looked at me like I was crazy and I quickly realized that *"musag"* may not actually mean "wristwatch".

When calling to make a doctor's appointment I asked for a *bedikat shed* (demon examination) instead of *bedikat shad* (breast examination).

My relative was trying to ask a butcher for chicken bottoms, and he said, "Do you have '*tachtonim*'?" which means, "Do you have underwear?"

At the store, I wanted to ask for *"shemen zayit"* (olive oil) but instead I asked for *"shemen zayin"* (penis oil)!

I was trying to buy chicken breast at the supermarket and

saw nothing to point to, so, pointing in the general direction of my breasts, I asked for "*ofe shadayim*," which means "chicken boobs." The butcher laughed, and I left with nothing.

A friend dropped her sock onto the neighbor's *mirpeset* (balcony) downstairs. She then knocked on the door and said that she came to get her "*gever*" (man) that fell, instead of saying her "*gerev*" (sock) that fell.

A friend's father asked for directions and then, instead of saying "*At bitucha*?" (which means, "Are you sure?") he said, "At *bitula*?" (which means, "Are you a virgin?").

My good friend was visiting Jerusalem and was on a bus. An old friend of hers – a religious man – saw her and said hi. She said, "Oh, I didn't recognize you with your pants ('*michnasayim*') on." She meant to say, "With your GLASSES ('*mishkifayim*') on!"

The first morning after giving birth to my first baby, I asked the midwives, "Where can I exchange the baby?" instead of "Where can I change the baby?"

I was shopping for underwear in Jerusalem, at some store that had samples under the glass top of a display case. Not seeing anything I liked, I tried asking the girl behind the counter if they had any other kinds. "*Yesh od min?*" I asked, in my awkward mix of modern and biblical Hebrew. She made that "tsk" sound that means no. Not knowing that tsk meant something, I thought she hadn't heard me and asked again. Another "tsk," only louder this time. I asked again. Irritated, she said, "I already answered you two times!" Only later did I found out what the word "*min*" means in modern Hebrew and that I had asked her, no less than three times, "Is there any more sex?"

A friend of mine asked for "*glulot*"(birth control pills) at a kiosk instead of "*gluyot*" (postcards). The answer she got was "*lo po, lo po*," "Not here, not here."

I always confuse "*adashim*" (lentils) and "*adashot*" (contact lenses) and end up asking if someone has lentils in their eyes!

I said to a shoe saleswoman when buying boots that my calf was "*shemenet*" (sour cream), instead of saying "*shemenah*," which means large or wide.

I spent a day once telling people that my *shadayim* really hurt me and did they want to take a look? (I meant *shkedim* – tonsils – as opposed to *shadayim*, which are breasts.) People were backing away in horror all day long.

I wanted to ask the sweet elderly Moroccan lady at work to water the little tree in the office. Instead of using the verb, *l'hashkot*, which means "to water," I used the verb *l'hashtin*, which means "to pee."

While at a boardroom meeting with 30 business people present, my friend's father wanted to say, "*Ani mamlitz al zeh*," which means "I recommend this." Instead, he said, "*Ani maflitz al zeh*," which means "I fart on this."

Israelifying

Olim Chadashim: The "Suckers" of the IDF

Shevi Zeff

Shevi was born in South Africa, and moved to Australia in 2001. After eleven years in a land down under, she made aliyah with her family to Israel, where she served in the search and rescue unit of the homefront command. Post-release, Shevi plans to work, travel, write and explore both the world around her and the country of her people. She looks forward to what the future holds.

The classic *oleh chadash* soldier story goes as follows: *Oleh chadash* thinks joining the IDF is top sh*t. *Oleh chadash* says, "Count me in!" and enlists to *Tzahal*. *Oleh chadash* goes for combat because it's the top of the top sh*t. *Oleh chadash* is given a gun and uploads a photo because now he is living the dream ... and has become that much cooler next to a gun. *Oleh chadash* has no idea what anyone is saying. *Oleh chadash* realizes – after one day of getting shouted at in words he doesn't understand, made to run laps around base, drop to do push-ups for any mistake, and eat canned rice-stuffed vine leaves that taste like butt – that he's made a huge mistake.

It hits him that he could have been on some beach drinking from a coconut in Bondi, Sydney – and instead, he's chugging a *mimia* (water bottle) in preparation for another *masa* (long intensive hike) and being timed by a commander who is at least a good three years younger than he is, yet holds all the power.

And that, folks, is why all *olim chadashim* are *friyarim* (suckers). That's more or less the joke that goes around in relation to those ignorant beings who decide to enlist in the IDF and serve this small desert country in the Middle East.

The number of times I've been called a sucker in the past two and a half years is probably not countable. Heck, the amount of times I've called myself a sucker for joining the IDF are probably equally not countable. The truth is that any dude who leaves a country of chilling and beach sides and nature and no worries in order to eat sh*t in Israel's IDF is a totally and wholesomely stupid young fool.

But you know what – I'll throw in a twist at this point with my good throwing hand (the right one, in case you were wondering) – speaking for myself, being a wholesomely stupid young fool has shaped my life in such a positive and significant way that even if you asked me in hindsight, knowing what I would go through, if I would join the IDF again, I wouldn't even blink twice – I'd choose to enlist every time.

Well, I hope you've come prepared for this, because I'm gonna open up a can (left handed – I like to mix things up) of reasons why stupid *olim chadashim* like yours truly gave up on the good life for the Defense Forces of this little desert country.

ahem ahem

Number one is the fact that Israel is the country that keeps us Jewish folk alive and athrive (that's not a word, but it sounded good). Honestly, knowing our history of being stepped on, pursued, slaughtered and beaten down – the fact that we have this God-given country as a country of our own is a means for us to stabilize our existence in this world. And when a country keeps us going, we reciprocate and see the need to keep it going … and I reckon finding that means of giving back through the IDF is a pretty good start, in my humble opinion. We have Israel, Israel has us.

Continuing on in that direction – even if the individual in his service simply eats shit and guards borders non-stop without any real action for the duration of his three years – the very fact that he has given of his time and sleep and freedom for the good of making sure things stay quiet on the home front is significant enough for him to know that in the time that he served, he played his part to the best of his ability for the holistic good of the nation. And, as *olim chadashim,* that sense of connection to a land we weren't born in, but defended with our lives – builds a strong relationship between us and our homeland that doesn't always come naturally to your average new immigrant.

Another game changer is Israeli culture: an *oleh chadash's* army adventure opens up a world of culture, language, and experiences with a richness that can't be spent on the market. Said *oleh chadash* will master the tongue of the people … after making a total fool of himself for a good few months (or years). He'll be blabbering Israeli slang and cranking up arsi music and pretending that he can sing with the intonations of Mizrachi singers. He'll be cursing his friends in Hebrew and writing "חחחח" in place of "lol." He'll be going out to hummus bars on Fridays and smoking *nargilah* on the beach in between games of *matkot* and bites of fresh watermelon with Bulgarian cheese (I still don't get it – but it's kinda delish). He'll hit up Israeli night life with army friends who have become, with time, blood brothers to him.

He'll see himself ease into the culture around him like a hand in a glove and his sense of belonging to this land and its people will feel completely natural to him. The barriers between his English-speaking background and new Israeli life will dissolve around him with time and he'll become a part of something greater than himself – of *Am Yisrael* in *Eretz Yisrael*. And this sounds cheesy as Gouda, but my IDF service has made this transition feel so natural and has given me so much in these critical foundational years of my life in Israel. And I can only be grateful for that.

And my final point for the day (because if I don't stop here, I'll just keep digging up new reasons, and you'll be reading this till your eyes get tired … or, alternatively, will stop reading, heaven forbid) is what said *oleh chadash* gets from the *tafkid* (role) he plays in his service. From being pushed to the limits and then pushed further in intensive training, to finding solace in the silence of 12-hour guard duty on the side of a highway in the Shomron – the experiences a soldier receives from his service are like no other and the things he learns from these experiences are significant to his building of a sense of self. An *oleh chadash* will join the army as one person, and leave it a changed person – because the nature of the service is so. It shapes who you are, teaches you your limits and capabilities, and a million other things you didn't know about yourself – and becomes a part of you. I think, for me, even when I get released, there's no doubt that my service will have impacted my life tremendously and, thank God, it's been (mostly) for the positive.

I really honestly could keep writing because I'm on a roll here – but I think my point has more or less been made for you, Mr. or Mrs. Reader. My point is that the totally stupid young fool who joined the IDF when he could've been slurping down a Tooheys New in the calm, peaceful terrain of Byron Bay, is not, in fact, an entirely stupid young fool. His pursuit of something greater than himself, and inner desire to give of himself for the good of a nation, country, religion and people is so significant an act. It's a life-changing service, a roller coaster of heaven and hell; an eye-opening, mind-challenging, physically intensive, and completely significant period of time that shapes one's identity and feeling of belonging as a citizen of this crazy beautiful country in the Middle East. I know, for me, despite all the hard times and moments of "why the heck am I doing this?!", I can only be grateful for the service that has been my gateway to a fantastic life (*bli ayin hara*) in a country that I can now wholeheartedly call my own, a country that will always remain, for me, a land flowing with milk and honey.

In Israel, I am Espresso and Bitter Chocolate

Sarah Tuttle-Singer

Sarah lives in Israel with her two kids and cat, in a village next to rolling fields. Sarah is the New Media Editor at The Times of Israel – the fastest growing news site on Israel. She writes about her life for a variety of places, including TOI, Kveller, *TIME.com* and Jezebel, and is working on her first book. She loves talking to strangers and exploring the complex and wonderful country she is making her home. Sarah made aliyah in 2010.

In LA, I am a vanilla latte (extra foam, please – oohhh and a chocolate chip muffin!).

I am strawberry margaritas with a light ring of salt, and a side order of fries (please and thanks). I am Champagne brunches with my BFF, henna tattoos, and dinners with family.

I am in bed by 11.

I am paperback books and framed photos from my childhood – the drawings my mother saved tucked away, and the diary I hid in a Ziploc bag beneath the orange tree in our backyard.

I am reruns.

I am rhinestone flip flops.

I am peaceful. (Sometimes bored.)

In LA, I am home.

And in Israel, I am espresso and bitter chocolate. I am whiskey neat and messy hair. I am catching rides and flying past fields on a purple bicycle.

I am climbing fig trees with my kids.

I am zeros and I am ones, phone calls at 2 a.m. I am notes typed in the middle of the night – up too late to make it to brunch in the morning – but there's always time for coffee or a drink, and chocolate croissants with the kids.

I am 18 browser tabs open at one time. I am a teal moleskin journal and a pen given to me at a train station.

I am the woman behind the camera, not in a frame.

I am working, digging, building, and tearing down to start all over, to make it better, to repair and piece together – building a home worth staying in that may never exist.

I am exhilarated. (I am exhausted.)

In Israel, I am the journey, not the destination.

I Want to Tell You About My Israel

Sarah Tuttle-Singer

I want to tell you about my Israel:

My blossoming, resilient, compassionate, progressive, brave Israel.

My Israel is farmers who speak Hebrew and farmers who speak Arabic, who work the land with sturdy hands, who just want to see things grow.

My Israel is the Rabbis for Human Rights who cross checkpoints to plant olive trees.

And the young woman who owns the flower shop on Dizengoff, and donates flowers to the funerals of terror victims.

And boys and girls who plant trees on Tu B'shvat, hoping one day they will use the branches for their own wedding canopies.

And an old woman who plants a seed deep into the earth, to grow a fig tree she'll never see beyond a dark green shoot – and that's only if she's lucky. But she plants it anyway, because one day her granddaughter will have a granddaughter, and she will gather figs and taste how sweet it is.

My Israel is rolling green fields, and orchards, cactus and clementines, a field of sunflowers in June, and the desert blooming red with poppies as soon as the rains fall. My Israel is lupine in the spring, and jasmine sweet on a warm night, it's tumbleweed, too – ragged and rolling, and a reminder to appreciate when the earth turns green again. Which it will. It always does.

My Israel is resilient and pushes limits.

My Israel is the three best friends who say, "Screw Algebra II," and skip class and go to the beach, because it's a gorgeous day outside and they're already smart enough to know that you can learn more outside the classroom sometimes.

My Israel is the 83-year-old man with a number tattooed on his arm, who wakes up every morning at sunrise and runs in Park HaYarkon, who *will* run the marathon this spring.

My Israel is the single mother who works full-time and goes to pharmacy school, who races home to tuck her babies in and sing them the same song her mother once sang to her, and then drinks two cups of coffee before she begins studying for her chemistry final.

My Israel is the boy with his hand in the air who always asks questions, and the girl who talks back to the teacher when the teacher is unfair, who stands up for her friends at recess, and who will one day stand up for her people as a leader in her own right.

And the doctor who gets on a plane after Hurricane Katrina and flies across the world to help heal the injured and rebuild an entire city all over again. My Israel is the hundreds of volunteers who are first in and last out.

My Israel remembers the Flood, and looks for the olive branch.

MY ISRAEL IS COMPASSIONATE.

My Israel is the bus driver who pulls over in the middle of a dust storm and insists that the woman walking by the side of the road get in and ride for free.

And the taxi driver who drove my children and me to the

hospital when my son couldn't breathe, who refused to take money for the ride, and, instead, handed me a string of prayer beads and a blessing on my son's head.

My Israel are the men and women who drive to army bases in a harsh winter storm with tureens of vegetable soup and hot chocolate and coffee for the soldiers who are out there braving the cold.

And the teenagers who volunteer at an orphanage and teach kids how to read.

And the tired soldier who gives up his seat on the bus for the pregnant woman in the hijab, and the man in the keffiyeh who drops a few coins into a beggar's cup by the Jerusalem bus station.

My Israel is the human rights workers who spend their lives defending the disenfranchised and the downtrodden, regardless of race or religion. My Israel does the right thing.

My Israel is potential.

My Israel is Shlomit and Moshe and Suha and Muhammad, who send their kids to a mixed Jewish and Arab school at Neve Shalom Wahat Al Salaam – Oasis of Peace. And my Israel is their two children, who share snack during recess.

My Israel is the sheikh on the Mount of Olives who welcomes weary travelers from all faiths, from all backgrounds, so long as they come with an open mind … and better yet, an open heart.

My Israel is those two women kissing in the middle of that rainbow crosswalk in Tel Aviv, and the two men who have adopted their first child from India, and welcome him into the tribe with family and friends to bear witness.

My Israel drives down to the desert to make it bloom, develops drip line irrigation sprinklers, and builds new power grids.

My Israel is the punk-ass kid in high school, who gets his

shit together in the army, then decides to start a company out of nowhere. And succeeds.

My Israel is a priest, an imam and a rabbi who all walk into a cafe to talk about faith and God – and no, this isn't the beginning of a joke. It's the beginning of a friendship.

My Israel is the people who show up when it's uncomfortable, when it's painful, when it's scary:

- The people who show up to a mosque desecrated by Jewish extremists because *"kol Yisrael arevim zeh la-zeh –* All of Israel is responsible for one another" doesn't just mean we have to have each other's backs. It means we have to take responsibility for the mistakes of our own people, too. These are the people who take brushes and soap and water and scrub walls, and then repaint to try to make it better.

- The people who show up to a demonstration with their children, even though it's late at night and crowded and hot and humid in the middle of summer, but they show up anyway, because it's important and they bring their tired children, too, because it's even MORE important for them to see what change can look like.

- The people who may come to blows with you over a parking space at Azrieli, but will show up at your uncle's funeral and wrap you in a warm, safe hug.

The people who run TOWARD a terror attack and not away from it, because they want to help to heal, to save lives if they can.

And sometimes, my Israel drives me up the freaking wall.

It's loud and way too close, and it pushes and shoves. It shouts and struggles and complains.

And it makes me want to pull my hair out at times, or go far away, to a place of quiet sunsets on an uncomplicated hill.

Sometimes, my Israel makes mistakes and forgets our history – where we've been, and more importantly, where we need to go.

But my Israel is so much more than that:

We are a work in progress. And just as Jacob wrestled with God to become Israel, so we in Israel wrestle with our own identity. For we are still a young country built on an ancient dream.

But, sometimes, I worry my Israel is in trouble – that forces of extremism and rigidity and intolerance will make the Israel I love disappear.

But I know we will get it right.

Because my Israel gets tears in their eyes when they sing "HaTikvah."

Because my Israel is hope.

The Top 14 Facts They Forgot to Tell You About Aliyah

Neil Lazarus

> Neil is an internationally acclaimed expert in the field of Middle East politics, Israeli public diplomacy and effective communication training. He is the director of AwesomeSeminars.com. Neil made aliyah in 1988.

The Jewish Agency and Nefesh B'Nefesh entice world Jewry to make aliyah with a list of promises and a smattering of rhetoric.

Now, for the first time, I present "The top 14 facts they forget to tell you about aliyah."

FACT ONE
Your children will be Israeli. A small detail, but important. Not only will they be first-generation sabras, they will laugh at your Hebrew, correct your grammar and wonder why you demand they use such words as "please" and "thank you."

FACT TWO
Within five years, your Hebrew will not get better, but your English will become worse. You will be unable to speak any language correctly before 8.30 a.m. Hint – invest in a good spell checker.

FACT THREE
If you are English, South African, Australian or just overweight,

you will be considered American by Israelis. I made aliyah from England to become an American, or "Anglo."

Fact Four
Forget ulpan; Israelis will speak English to you.

Fact Five
Hebrew doesn't sound right when spoken with an English accent.

Fact Six
Within five years, you will not be able to wait in a line. Elbows will have never-before-thought-of uses.

Fact Seven
You will look at your bank statement to check how much you don't have in your account. The larger your overdraft, the more successful the aliyah. The statement "the way to make a small fortune in Israel is to come with a big one" will become less funny as reality sinks in.

Fact Eight
If you make aliyah in your twenties, you will have endless friends staying with you from abroad, having discovered cheap accommodation in Israel. Within ten years, they will have forgotten you. Search in the David Citadel Hotel; you will find them there.

Fact Nine
Cars are taxed at 100%, Cadbury's chocolate just isn't the same in Israel, and EastEnders is two weeks behind Britain. (Americans, just remember the 100%.)

Fact Ten
You will wear sandals for five years, feeling like a combination of a Sabra and Jesus, only to realize that there are more comfortable options.

Fact Eleven
News from other countries will come to seem inane.

Fact Twelve
Within five years, you will "tut" instead of saying no, and you will drive in a way you would never have believed.

Fact Thirteen
You will shout at a traffic cop. I promise you, you will.

Fact Fourteen
Despite all of the above, your children will be Jewish and will have a sense of pride. You will walk the roads where Jewish prophets and kings once walked. You will celebrate Jewish holidays and walk streets named after mega-Jews – not saints. You will become a part of Jewish history as it unfolds, and, as an Israeli, you will be a Jew – not Jew*ish*.

Discovering My Inner Israeli

Rebecca Bermeister

Rebecca was born in South Africa, grew up in Australia, and now lives in Israel where she blogs about the challenges of life in the Middle East. While juggling motherhood, writing, therapy, and homeopathy, Rebecca recently published her first book, *Waiting for Kate*, a tale of melancholy, motherhood, sisterhood and love, set in a small village in the Middle East, where tea cups line the balcony. Pieces from her blog, *An Aliyah Journal*, have been published in Australian and Israeli news publications.

This year marks our family's four year aliyah anniversary, and much as I hate to admit it, in some strange ways, Israel is starting to feel like home. As I drive from our home town of Zichron Ya'akov down the winding hills through Binyamina and on to the flatlands of Pardes Hanna, I now recognize fields and landmarks as if I had grown up amongst them. I know how to avoid the morning traffic and still get the kids to school on time. I know the shortcuts and the back roads, and I know the one-way streets even though the signs are covered with foliage. I am comforted by that old familiar feeling of knowing an area well enough to give directions to strangers who suddenly stop in the middle of the road, oblivious to the seven cars waiting impatiently behind them.

When I step onto the pedestrian crossing and confidently march across the street, admittedly risking my life, I feel like I have conquered something within. I have developed a strength of character, a certain don't mess with me, I'm Israeli attitude expressed effortlessly through my body language.

I have even taken on the queue. For many years, I just waited and observed. What else was there to do when the Moroccan woman behind me had an elbow as sharp as a knife and the voice of a man? But this year, it seems I have given birth to a ferocious inner being; I have embraced my inner Israeli.

Last week, I met a friend for our regular early morning coffee at a local gas station (yes, we Israelis like our coffee with our gas, go figure). As I was standing at the counter, a relatively normal-looking guy projected his order for coffee across the crowd of people waiting to be served. I turned my body to face him and simply asked, "How can you do that? What makes you think your time is more important than ours?" He immediately admitted I was right (though not that he was wrong), and I proceeded to order our coffee while he waited patiently. I asked my friend for the equivalent expression in Hebrew – *"Lama kacha?"* which means, "Why like this?" and which, in all honesty, better suits my Anglo sensibilities. Since then, I throw it around at every opportunity I get, which is often.

Another habit I have come to accept is that, generally speaking, the first reaction of many Israelis in the service industry is no, it's not possible. But if you show a little stamina, and some power of reason, they will usually, albeit begrudgingly, be swayed to saying yes. My favorite example being the sales operator from Apple who insisted that the only way I could collect my small purchase was to come pick it up myself. When she asked for my address (to direct me to their nearest store), I told her I lived on the moon and there was no way I could possibly get there. Still she insisted, no delivery service. It's not possible, she said. This is Apple, Israel, 2012, I told her, it's not possible that it's not possible. I asked to talk to her manager, and of course she came back to me with a yes. The parcel was delivered to my house within a few days.

When I asked the women behind the counter at the Misrad Hapanim (Ministry of the Interior) for a new plastic sleeve for my ID papers, her immediate response was a firm no. She wanted me to bring in the old one to exchange it. For a moment, I was excited, thinking the Interior Ministry had embarked on a recycling campaign, but even if that were that the case, which believe me, it wasn't, my newfound inner Israeli was not so easily intimidated. I looked her squarely in the eyes and said, "Are you really asking me to drive all the way home to find my old plastic cover at the bottom of the garbage bin and then bring it back to you before you give me a new one?" She turned the corners of her mouth up and reluctantly handed me a shiny new plastic sleeve, which I thanked her for in Hebrew and left.

It takes a certain abrasive confidence to deal with Israelis every day, since many of them have little sense of personal space or regard for personal boundaries. Perhaps their mothers were too busy working, defending the state, or surviving to teach them not to push into a queue or not to make a turn without indicating. But I am starting to get the hang of it. Now that I have laid claim to my own inner Israeli, I feel that it's both my right and my duty to teach them how to behave at every opportunity I can, which only goes to prove the point.

The First for Our First: *Tzav Rishon*

Romi Sussman

> When Romi isn't working on her professional or personal writing, you'll find her running after six sons ages 6–16. Romi made aliyah in 2004 from Potomac, Maryland and has been thriving in the hills of Gush Etzion every since.

At 16, I came to Israel on a teen tour. I enjoyed the six-week experience, the tour of the country, and the beauty of the Land. And then I went home. But something had stuck, had connected, had pulled me. I returned as a 20-year-old college student, and then for a year in a post-college program.

Each time, there were many things that struck me, stuck with me, made me choke up. But perhaps none more so than the soldiers that I saw. I remember thinking to myself – these kids are the same age that I am. And if I believe in the State of Israel – if I believe that it should exist and continue existing – then why should they be serving and I shouldn't be? Why is that fair?

The years trickled by, or flew by, as they sometimes do, and I was raising two beautiful little boys in Maryland. As we started to think about how we wanted to raise them, who we wanted them to be, it was hard to get away from the Zionist calling.

People said, "Are you crazy? You know they are going to have to be in the army one day, right?"

I didn't quite understand them. Yes, I would think. That's

exactly it. Why should I be raising my boys to love Israel, to respect Israel, to want an Israel to exist... but not to have to be part of that experience? To not be part of that commitment?

Of course the story ends, or begins, with our aliyah.

But now, those two beautiful boys are not so little, and they have been joined by four brothers. Yes, I've known in the most metaphorical and theoretical sense that someday I would have to stick by that commitment, to the conviction that I had, that I would have to lend my boys to the army.

When the day comes, however, it's no longer theoretical. The dawning of that first day came on Friday when my oldest got his *tzav rishon* (first call up to the army) in the mail. The feeling was like none that I've experienced before. Well, perhaps it was akin to the day we boarded the plane to make aliyah. We knew we were doing the right thing for ourselves; we were excited and enthusiastic, bright-eyed and eager. And yet, there was a part of me giving pause. We were leaving everything behind and taking a leap of faith that seemed crazy – and yet natural as well. It was terrifying and exciting, gratifying and completely nerve-wracking.

The feelings of pride and anticipation didn't erase the fear, worry and apprehension.

My son groaned when I wanted to take a picture of him with his *tzav rishon*. "Mommy," he said while trying to check his phone and eat, "It's just the first paperwork. It's nothing. Everyone gets it."

Yes, sweetheart, everyone gets it. And that, as well, is a miracle to me. I don't believe I'll ever stop seeing the miracle as long as I live here. It's amazing to me that he sees it as no big deal, as just something that everyone does, as a commitment that he will obviously be making. A no-brainer.

I see it as an amazing commitment. A chance to join with his people and connect to thousands of years of history – through his body and his being. And while he takes it for granted because it's all he knows, I never will.

My grandfather, Jerry Weinhouse, was the last person in my family to don a uniform. He fought for America in World War II, earning two purple hearts. And now, his first grandson will be putting on a uniform that didn't exist when he was fighting the Nazis. A uniform that was just a dream, a 2,000-year-old prayer.

And that is now a reality. Our reality.

Like Dreamers

Dov Lipman

Rabbi Dov Lipman was elected to the 19th Knesset with the Yesh Atid party, making him the first American born MK in 30 years. He holds rabbinic ordination from Ner Israel Rabbinical College and a master's in education from Johns Hopkins University. Rabbi Lipman is the author of five books about Judaism and Israel and moved to Israel with his wife and four children in July 2004.

If someone would have approached me when I descended the steps from my aliyah flight in July 2004 and told me that within 10 years I would become a member of the Knesset, I would have simply laughed. First of all, I had no political aspirations. I was thrilled to have been hired to teach Torah in post high school gap year programs for English-speaking young adults. Second, I was not anywhere close to being fluent in Hebrew and I had no plans to take ulpan since I didn't need Hebrew for my profession. Finally, I had seen on the news that the political culture in Israel was quite intense, with leaders regularly interrupting one another and even screaming, and I was a quiet and polite American who said please and excuse me and raised my hand to ask permission to speak in public venues.

But Israel was built on the belief that the impossible can come true – with God's help – and there I was, in January 2013, being sworn in as a member of Knesset with the new Yesh Atid party led by Yair Lapid. I had gotten involved in some issues which developed in my hometown of Beit Shemesh, and that community work brought me into the Israeli political world.

Without a doubt, my greatest challenge upon entering the Knesset was the Hebrew language. I was petrified of functioning in the Hebrew-speaking world of the Knesset, especially given the public nature of the position and its responsibilities. One breakthrough moment came in my first live television interview on Channel Two's prime time news. I was not in the studio and could only hear the anchorwoman in my earpiece. I struggled my way through – no doubt consistently mixing up masculine and feminine terms – and breathed a sigh of relief as the interview concluded and the news went to a commercial break. Once off air, the anchorwoman asked me, "How long have you been in Israel?" I replied, "Since 2004," and she responded, "Such a short time? Your Hebrew is fantastic." I knew that it wasn't, but this moment taught me that Israelis don't expect our Hebrew to be perfect. They appreciate the fact that we are new immigrants trying to speak Hebrew. We should never be afraid of speaking Hebrew with Israelis.

One may ask: If Israelis appreciate that we are trying to speak Hebrew, why do they always answer our Hebrew with English? Every person reading this who has tried to speak Hebrew in Israel knows precisely what I am referring to. Doesn't this demonstrate that our Hebrew is atrocious and we should not even bother?

The answer is a clear no. I have learned that Israelis answer us in English for one of two reasons. Either they want to show that they know English or they want to practice their English. The latter was true for me in the Knesset. Colleagues, from the Prime Minister to security guards, spoke to me in English and my fellow MKs explained that they were simply taking advantage of an opportunity to practice their English.

Despite the fact that the Israelis were completely understanding of my weak Hebrew, delivered in a heavy American accent, I decided to make history. Every MK is given a budget to study a second language. Most use it for English. Some choose Russian and some Arabic. I became the first Knesset member to use this budget for Hebrew. Every Sunday, I met with my tutor, Nadav, who tortured me as he pushed me to master Hebrew grammar along with the vocabulary unique to the Knesset. We watched my speeches together and he ripped them apart, correcting every mistake. And the tutoring worked. After a few months, I was far more comfortable and confident and my Hebrew improved remarkably.

My biggest fear was that I would say a wrong word in a speech and end up the laughingstock of the Knesset on political satire shows. Fortunately, with thanks to God and a lot of preparation before my speeches, I only confused one word. When praising the first ultra-Orthodox woman to serve as a dean in an Israeli university, I called her a "daikanit" – someone who is very precise" – instead of a "dikanit" – a dean. Thank God it was not too bad a mistake.

All of this taught me that English speaking immigrants should throw themselves into speaking Hebrew – despite our accent and despite our mistakes and even if Israelis answer in English. Do Ulpan. Find a tutor. Do whatever is necessary to be the best that you can be and recognize that mistakes and imperfections are accepted as part of living in a country of immigrants.

The Knesset culture and the way MKs argue with one another was something I had to adapt to. I will never forget when, in committee, another MK was saying something which I strongly disagreed with and a fellow party member was pushing me to say something. He leaned over and said, "Bang on the table and scream out that you disagree." It took me some time to build up the courage, but then I did it. And the room went silent. The quiet and respectful American had spoken out, and the surprise drew significant attention to what I had to say.

This also taught me another important lesson. We don't have to change who we are or our nature to succeed in Israel. But every once in a while, a little bit of Israeli chutzpah and toughness may be called for and when that time comes – just go for it!

English speakers have so much to contribute to Israeli society and we can help make Israel an even greater country. We have to put aside our fears and just roll up our sleeves and get involved. Speaking Hebrew isn't easy, but you can do it. Adjusting to Israeli culture isn't easy. But you can do it. Making changes in the country is not easy, but we can do it. The list of challenges that come with making aliyah and becoming an essential part of Israel is long. But they can be overcome. We live in the most remarkable of times, in which God has blessed us with our homeland, and no one should think that they cannot make it in Israel. Whenever things get tough on a personal or professional level, I remind myself of something that happened to me thirty years ago.

As a young teenager in Silver Spring, Maryland, my school bussed us to Washington, DC a few times to demonstrate across from the Soviet embassy on behalf of Soviet Jewry – our brothers and sisters who were trapped behind the Iron Curtain. One of those times, on a cold Washington winter day, we held a silent vigil and were given signs to hold up. My sign said, "Free Yuli Edelstein."

"*Shir ha'maalot beshuv HaShem et shivat tzion hayinu k'chol'mim.*" King David teaches that when the people of Israel return to Zion, "We are like dreamers."

Thirty years after that moment, I was blessed to sit as a member of the Knesset, and Yuli Edelstein was the speaker of the Knesset. Thirty years beforehand, I was a regular American teenager not thinking about living in Israel, while Yuli was languishing away in prison cell in Siberia. But in these most magnificent of times, 30 years later, we were reunited in the Jewish state, in the Jewish capital, in the Jewish parliament.

We are all blessed to live in the best of times, in which nothing is impossible, and the land of Israel is ours and available for all Jews to settle, raise their families, and contribute to its future and the future of the Jewish people. "We are like dreamers." The time is now for all of us to turn dreams into reality.

An Immigrant's Tale

Tamar Kane

Originally from New York, Tamar graduated from Northwestern University in 2013. Following graduation, she made aliyah with Garin Tzabar and enlisted in the IDF as a combat fitness instructor in Golani. She currently lives in Tel Aviv and is pursuing course work towards a degree in nutrition.

It is one of those days in Tel Aviv. The sun beats down on you, taunting you, blinding you and making you question your sanity.

I duck into my favorite coffee shop, seeking refuge. I sit down, exhaling. A figure stirs in the corner of my vision, and someone asks if they can slip in next to me. I recognize the well-worn look of a member of that tribe that experiences the agony of wanderlust. Roaming from country to country, shedding parts and rearranging others as he goes. He sits beside me, taking in the scene. Nodding his head slightly with a half-smile at the young Israelis milling about in their fashionable haircuts, like he gets it. He asks me which way to the markets. Our accents and easy banter make it clear that we are from the same part of the world. Immediate allies.

At first, I give him the practiced and polished version, the one I know by heart from constant reuse. It has become like a favorite go-to shirt, one I reach for automatically because I know it will do the trick. It is the shortened telling that will elicit just the right amount of interest, but not too much, God forbid he should delve in too far. Not because I don't want to share. Or because it makes me uncomfortable. Some things are just impossible to explain.

I lay down the facts: I'm 25. I moved to Israel three years ago. I graduated from college. My family still lives in New York. I joined the army, traveled around Southeast Asia, and here I am. In this coffee shop.

He shrugs his shoulders with that twinkle in his eye that people often get when I give them this narrative.

"Would you say that it's easy to fit in, like you've become Israeli? Or do you always feel like an American on the outside?"

Something about his focused stare, the deep nod with the closed eyes, tells me I can share. He understands. He has been here.

I mentally reel through video clips of memory.

I am in the army. The Israeli elections are coming up, and the air is rife with controversial debates. Each person fervently feels that his opinion is the right one. I am sitting at a picnic table outside with some commanders I know, and some I do not. Their comments offend me, and I offer up a counterargument. One that I do not know looks at me with scorn and spits, "How would you know? You weren't here during the Intifada. You don't have friends who were killed."

I recoil. From the aggression in his voice, and because he is right about my not being here. That doesn't make my opinion less valid. But I recognize that it is not tinged with a native Israeli's experiences and history. It reminds me of lochamim, *combat soldiers, one-upping each other's service. "I closed Shabbat." "Well I closed 21 days on base." "You think that's bad? I haven't left base in two months ..."*

You don't know struggle.

I am in a Chabad house in India. We emerge from between the emaciated cows, the jerky tuk-tuks, and the merciless sun, gathering here to feel a sense of home. An Israeli with a curly mop on his head

and scars along his arms asks me where in Israel I live. I turn to say
something to my friend in English.

He furrows his brow.

"Why is your English so good?"

"I'm American."

"But you don't even have an accent, achoti. *Sister. You're Israeli."*

The petite girl next to him asks what I did in the army. Her eyes
light up. "I did that, too! You must know Yael, or Maya, or Shira,
they were in the course with me…" From within this tiny country,
of course we find connections.

This identity crisis becomes constant conversation while
my friend, also American-born, and I travel. Completing the
post-army rite of passage.

We are walking down a narrow, crowded alleyway in Vietnam,
our hiking bags strapped to our backs, our sweaty hair matted to our
faces. We warily glance around at the hostel options, when we hear
a snippet of conversation: "Ha-achsania hazot niret sababa. *This*
hostel looks good." We nod at each other and go inside, knowing we
have found comrades. The Israelis checking in glance at our shoresh
sandal-clad feet, the symbol of the Israeli traveler.

"Az miefo aten? So where are you from?"

We glance at each other, silently conversing with our eyes. You
take this one. I took the last one.

"We live in Israel, but we were born in New York…"

Where are we from? We feel the need to explain our lineage
every time. Yes, we speak Hebrew. Yes, we were in the army. Yes,
we went to an American university, and no, it is not like *American Pie*. We have an immediate connection with these people,
a kinship. Yet we feel like impostors claiming complete *sabra*
status, yet compelled to add the born-in-America addendum.

I look back at my fellow American in my favorite coffee
shop in Tel Aviv.

An image surfaces in my mind of one of my soldiers, his olive uniform drenched a dark forest green with sweat. He is limping over to me at the end of his *masa kumta*, the 70-kilometer hike after which soldiers receive berets and complete the first stage of training. He looks at me and says in exhausted awe, "Tamar, *ba'ima sheli*, on my mother, you should get a *sikat lochem*."

That's the pin fighters get upon completing their training. But I wasn't born a fighter. I just chose to be one.

Isn't there a difference?

Celebrating Israel's Birthday

Yael Eckstein

Yael is Senior Vice President of the International Fellowship of Christians and Jews where she oversees all ministry programs and serves as the international spokesperson for the $140 million organization. She is a regular contributor to *The Jerusalem Post* and author of two books, *Holy Land Reflections: A Collection of Inspirational Insights from Israel* and *Spiritual Cooking with Yael*. In addition, she can be heard weekly on The Fellowship's radio program *Holy Land Moments*, which airs on over 1,500 radio stations around the world. Yael made aliyah in 2005.

I have never been one to make a big deal about birthdays, but celebrating the birth of my homeland is an exception.

As the sun set on Remembrance Day – the day we remember Israel's fallen soldiers and victims of terrorism – and Jewish people around the world wiped the tears from their eyes to make way for the unadulterated joy and thanksgiving we feel on Independence Day, I felt exhilarated.

After an intense day of attending Remembrance Day events at my children's school, sitting with my neighbor who lost her youngest son in the 2006 Second Lebanon War, and listening to countless heroic war stories, I felt ready and anxious to celebrate this amazing land that I am blessed to call home.

When the clock struck 8 p.m., my husband and I packed our three flag-waving children into the car, blasted traditional Israeli music, and made our way to the communal *Hallel* (thanksgiving) prayers. As I watched hundreds of people sing, dance, and thank God for the greatest gift bestowed to the Jews in thousands of years – our beloved land of Israel – I felt deeply emotional.

My Sabra friends watched tears fill my eyes at the communal singing of "Hatikva," the national anthem, and seemed puzzled. "Since I'm a relatively new immigrant, this is one of the most personally meaningful holidays of the year," I explained to them. They still seemed curious and somewhat confused, so I continued to tell them what was in my heart at that special moment.

"When you grow up outside Israel and make the decision to leave everything you know behind in order to fulfill your dream of moving to the Promised Land, Independence Day is not a holiday you take for granted," I said. "As someone who spent half of her life living outside of the Jewish homeland, it's the small details of life in Israel that are so moving and powerful for me."

With songs of Hallel coming through the loudspeaker, I sat down on the sandy earth and took a few moments to reflect on my deep love for Israel and her people.

I remembered how many times while living in the US I had longed to walk on the cobblestone streets of Jerusalem. As I prayed the "Grace after meals" blessing, I would plead, "Have mercy Lord, our God, on Jerusalem Your city, on Zion the resting place of Your glory, and rebuild Jerusalem, the holy city, soon in our days."

I remembered the synagogue of my youth, which was beautiful and full of kind and sweet people; and yet, I never felt a special spirit of redemption, a feeling that I only experience at prayer services in Israel.

I leaned back against an ancient tree, and took myself back to the day I got on the El Al flight with a one-way ticket to Israel.

I stepped onto that airplane in America confused and scared, yet by the time I arrived at my new apartment in Jerusalem, I felt a sense of peace like never before.

It was like a heavy weight had been lifted from my soul.

I made aliyah because of my deep-rooted belief that I was born into a special generation that has the blessing of calling Israel home after 2,000 years of exile, because of a profound faith that God performed miracles so that I could return to my roots, people, and land.

Sitting in my apartment in New York, each time I would second-guess my decision to make aliyah, I would remind myself: Moses only got to see the Land of Israel, while I have the ability to live there. How could I turn it down? Yes, these "big picture" ideals brought me to Israel, but it's been the small details of life in the Holy Land that have kept me a passionate Zionist, utterly in love with this once barren land that has bloomed before our eyes.

I love the street names, which are almost all named in honor of biblical heroes, founders of the nation of Israel, or philanthropists who helped develop the modern state.

I love the *savtot* (grandmothers) who spend their days reciting Tehillim (psalms) while sitting on park benches, in public buses and inside ancient synagogues.

I love the fact that my children are in school with Jewish kids from Ethiopia, Yemen, Morocco, Russia and many other places.

I love how people go to weddings in jeans and a button-down shirt.

I love how everyone feels like family to each other, creating an atmosphere where you can be blunt and speak your mind.

I love how when I take my babies for a walk, everyone on the street comes up to me with their opinion as to whether the baby is too cold or too hot.

I love how the people of Israel have diverse opinions on almost everything, yet everyone comes together in unity during times of celebration and hardships.

I love how the country shuts down for Jewish holidays, and how on Fridays even the radio broadcaster closes his show with "Shabbat Shalom."

I love taking family trips to biblical places like Beersheba, Jerusalem, and the Judean Hills, and studying the stories that took place there thousands of years ago.

Most of all, I love living in this country where every stone, hilltop, and flower is imbued with holiness and sanctity, with the story and heritage of my people.

I understand how people who were born and raised in Israel might think that I'm overly emotional and sentimental when I cry each time I hear "Hatikva" being sung, yet I pray that no matter how long I have lived in Israel, my heart never hardens to the magnificent reality experienced here, and to the divine blessing being bestowed upon us all each day we are able to call this Holy Land home.

Take Now My Son

Shira Pasternak Be'eri

Shira is a Jerusalem-based writer, editor, and translator. She is the website coordinator of the Mandel Foundation-Israel and the former editor of the Israel Democracy Institute's English website. Born and raised in New York, she has been living in Israel since 1982. She blogs at The Times of Israel.

This boy. This precious, long-awaited boy.

When his future arrival was still a secret, a careless driver collided with my car door. My hand instinctively flew to protect my belly, rather than to the dashboard to protect myself. Such is a mother's love.

This boy. This wondrous and magical boy.

When he was one, and I found myself in danger, fearing for my life, the thought of this golden-haired, blue-eyed boy carried me through, as I imagined his sparkling smile.

This boy. This even-tempered, rational boy.

When he was five, we saw him get angry for the very first time. A rumbling "moose call" welled up and burst out from inside him, and all we could do was laugh.

This boy. This generous and caring boy.

When he was 10, he stepped aside to make room for a foster brother a year his senior, graciously sharing all that was his, including the hardest thing of all: his parents.

This boy. This innovative, creative boy.

When he was 13, his tutorial for making paper rocket launchers was featured by a Lithuanian website, inspiring thousands of English-speaking teens.

This boy. This compassionate and peaceful boy.

When he was 16, his conscience clashed with his love of meat, and he became vegetarian 24/6, as part of a deal he made with the cows.

This boy. This modest and unassuming boy.

When he was 17, he designed a productivity app that has been downloaded more than 100,000 times. But he never let it go to his head.

This boy. This guitar-strumming, wood-working boy.

At 18, this sandy-haired, grey-eyed boy has broad shoulders, weathered hands, and long arms that are perfect for high-fives or a warm embrace.

And in the years in between, this boy filled our lives with wonder and adventure. He shared with us his loose teeth and scraped knees, K'nex contraptions and domino rallies, drum solos and cheek concertos. His life was full of bike rides and back flips, dog walking and doodling, roller coasters and wave boards, photography and art projects, culinary experiments and krav maga, judo and junk food. And, as he grew, his paper airplanes gave way to hackathons and stellar grades, and we learned to rely on his expertise in audio equipment and mobile phones.

But the IDF said: "Take now your son, your youngest son, the son you love, whose name means 'joy' and 'friendship,' and go to the place that I will show you and offer him to the service of his country."

And this boy, this gentle, caring boy, is being trained for combat.

Trembling, we wake up early in the morning and ascend to that place, and hand him over willingly, graciously, entrusting his care to something larger than we are as he gives up his autonomy.

We mourn his loss of freedom and our loss of our family as we know it, fearing for his safety, missing him already, knowing that he will be absent from many family occasions in the future.

Suddenly, we become Israeli in a different way, joining the ranks of parents who stop breathing for two or three or five or nine or eleven years, while waiting for their own "this boy" or "this girl" to come home.

I think of what I was doing when I was his age, and of what his peers are doing now in the United States. How would his life be different had I never made aliyah? I wonder if he would have preferred it that way.

As we force ourselves to separate, we curse the reality that demands that we send our sons and daughters to war, when we long to be beating our swords into plowshares. But at the very same time, our hearts swell with pride and soar with gratitude, as we look at our son in awe, and bless the reality in which we live in our own homeland and can take responsibility for our own defense.

This boy. This mild-mannered and moral boy.

What will the experience of the army do to his body? What will it do to his soul? How will his service impact what he does in his life and when he does it? How will it affect who he loves and when he loves? Which of his experiences will he share with us? What will we never know?

This boy. This buzz-cut, khaki-clad boy.

May God bless and keep this boy.

May God shine the divine light upon him and be gracious to him.

May God turn toward this boy and bring him home safely to this mom.

And may God grant him, and all of us, peace.

Becoming Israeli

Akiva Gersh

Before making aliyah, living in Israel seemed to me to be an almost exclusively spiritual act. During my pre-aliyah visits, I spent the majority of my time in Jerusalem and Tzfat, studying Torah and hanging out with friends who, like me, were also in Israel just hanging out. No one worked. No one was married yet. We were in Israel to soak up the holiness of the resurrected Jewish presence in the Holy Land. At any given moment, you could find us, in our big colorful kippot, with our tzitzit blowing in the wind, hiking to a natural spring, cooking vegetarian meals together, talking about G-d and playing music until two in the morning.

Upon making aliyah, I thought life here was going to be at least somewhat a reflection of those good ol' days. You could imagine how shocked I was when I very quickly realized that life in Israel wasn't just about getting ready for Shabbat! Amazingly enough, real life actually took place during the other six days of the week, meaning normal, worldly activities like working, food shopping, and paying bills were on the agenda.

Okay, so maybe I'm exaggerating a bit. But just a bit. One of my first surprises was when our landlord sent a technician to our house to explain how the heating system worked. "They have technicians in Israel??" was my first, albeit naïve, thought. To add to my disbelief, the guy showed up with a kippah on his head! I had never seen such a thing: a Jewish, religious technician! He was a super sweet guy and explained to us, in very beautiful and impressively fast Hebrew (with a Moroccan accent for dramatic effect), how the heating system worked. I just kept smiling at him, nodding my head as if to say, "Yup, I do indeed have no idea what you are saying." To myself I thought, "Rebbe Nachman never mentioned moments like this when he praised and extolled the virtues of living in the land of Israel."

It didn't take long until I realized that I was actually going to have to live a somewhat normal life in Israel. I also realized, however, that what was normal in Israel was quite different from what I had come to know as normal in America. Though I was moving to the Jewish state, a state built for Jews just like me, it still, in many ways, felt like a foreign country. In addition to this new language known as Modern Hebrew that I would have to learn, (see next blog), there were many other new things that I would need to get used to. Like driving on Israeli highways, standing in Israeli lines, speaking with Israeli salespeople and, most of all, raising kids who would, to my utter shock and surprise, actually be Israeli.

Let me make it very clear: I love Israelis. They inspire me and impress me and challenge me in all kinds of positive ways. And I love the fact that, since making aliyah in 2004, I have changed quite a bit living here. Things I never thought I would do, I now do. Things I never thought I could do, I learned I could do. Basically, I started becoming Israeli. In ways that even surprise me sometimes. But I have to say, I kinda like it. It strangely feels more … me.

So, in celebration of the often unexpected, personal transformations that olim go through after making aliyah, here's a list of telltale signs that you are, in fact, becoming more Israeli:

You overtake not one, not two, but even three cars on the highway at once.

Hitchhiking becomes another mode of transportation. Even when you're waiting for a bus, you stick out your finger just to see if someone stops.

Your 9-year-old daughter's play date says, "Shit!" and you don't flinch.

You can't think of a certain word in English even though it's your native tongue.

You don't want to hike in anything but sandals.

You start calling all kinds of strangers, *"Achi!"* ("My brother!")

You take a number at the bank/post office/*misrad*/whatever, but push in front anyway, because "I just want to ask a quick question."

You stop getting angry at every single car that cuts you off on the road. (There's too many for that.)

You can successfully be funny in Hebrew.

You legitimately forget to use the word "please" when speaking in English.

You ask random strangers how much they pay in rent. And how much money they earn from their job.

You bring inflatable mattresses, a generator, pots and pans, and lots more on a one-night camping trip.

You make that weird clicking noise with your tongue when you want to say, "No."

You show up to weddings in normal everyday clothes ... and, of course, sandals.

When asked at the store if you want to pay in payments, you enthusiastically say, "Yes!"

You text with your kids in Hebrew.

When people ask you for directions, you say, "Just go straight, straight, straight, the whole time, until ..."

You visit your country of origin and you feel like a foreigner.

You pick your nose in public.

You find yourself genuinely not noticing when you cut people in line.

You start eating *harif* (spicy sauce).

You start drinking Turkish coffee.

You say "*yofi*", "*yalla*", or "*sababa*" in almost every sentence.

You're shocked when you visit Port Authority in NYC and see 50 people standing patiently and happily in an organized line.

You can no longer tolerate smiley, friendly salespeople in stores during those same visits.

You love saying "*B'tayavon*" or "*La'briyut*" as you walk by a stranger eating food.

You don't leave phone messages anymore. If someone leaves you one, you don't listen to it.

You call back a missed call, even from a number you don't recognize.

You make all kinds of grammatical mistakes in English that you never used to make, saying things like, "You can eat OR pasta OR a sandwich."

You're considering buying a traveling coffee-making set. (If you actually purchased one, then you are super-Israeli.)

You bring less and less stuff back from America.

You bring Israeli products with you when you visit the States so your kids will have something to eat.

You finally understand how two mature and responsible grown-ups can have a negative account balance ("go into minus") by the end of the month.

You stop trying to avoid saying words in public that begin with the letter "*reish*".

You see an open spot on a sidewalk and it seems like a great (and totally legal) place to park your car. So you do.

You no longer tense up when someone starts to tell a joke

in Hebrew, worried that you won't get the joke and will be the only one not laughing.

Your Ashkenazi kids listen to Mizrachi music.

You finally start learning the words to the songs your kids sing in *gan* (kindergarten).

You accept the fact that your salary here is half of what you made in America and that many things cost twice as much. (Kind of.)

You finally understand how the Israeli government works. (Kind of.)

You finally allow yourself to sign all kinds of things, from store receipts to important documents, with just a *kishkush* (squiggle) instead of your full legible signature.

You start saying (a lot), "*Y'hiye beseder*" ("Everything will be okay") and fully believe it.

A View from Afar

Aliyah: A Sacrifice Too Big?

Hannah Dreyfus

Hannah is currently a staff writer for the *New York Jewish Week*, published online and in print and distributed to 60,000+ households weekly. There, she investigates and reports on trends among Jewish youth and millennials, Orthodox politics and culture, and Reform and Conservative Jewish life. She is the Project Manager for the *Jewish Week*'s Investigative Journalism Fund, an initiative to fill a gap in investigative reporting in the Jewish world. She lives with her husband in Brooklyn, NY.

Date question: So – feelings about aliyah?

For some, the question is a deal breaker. For most, it's a discussion.

Within the Modern Orthodox community, the question is rarely one of *loving* Israel. Our allegiance is assumed, our reverence expected. Israeli flags in dorm rooms and teary eyes during the recital of "HaTikvah" serve as mere confirmations. We dance on Yom HaAtzmaut and cry on Yom HaZikaron. We visit for holidays and reminisce generously about our seminary and yeshiva experiences, traipsing around the cobble-stoned streets of Jerusalem.

But who's going back?

Those who answer *deal breaker* have chosen Israel. But those of us who finagle around the question of aliyah, talking about jobs and family ties and war-zones? We've chosen America.

I don't make light of these considerations. I don't make light of the decision to stay in the United States. What I find interesting, however, is the way we acknowledge the decision we have made to stay in America. More often than not, the challenge to verbalize the decision is accompanied by justifications, rationalizations, ambivalence, and even shame.

We justify: We're here, yes. But our hearts are with Israel. We proudly display *"Libi ba'mizrach"* (*"My heart is in the East"*) quotations on necklaces, rings, and bracelets. We assiduously keep up with the news, visit when we can, and add the names of soldiers to our daily prayers. But are we going? Make no mistake: Aliyah is no passive choice. It is a dream that has to be prioritized. No choice is the tacit agreement to stay here.

When the aliyah question is addressed to me, my response is wrought with ambivalence. When I am posed with the question, I longingly recall the unique experience of being a Jew in Israel. I recall the *chag sameach* greeting signs on buses, the taxi driver who handed me a small book of *Tehillim* and told me to recite after him, the elementary school children at Shabbat tables who could recite entire sections of *Chumash* by heart. I respond that aliyah is an ideal. A far off dream, perhaps – but a dream no less vivid.

However, the pronouncement of aliyah as an unequivocal ideal is quickly followed up by a laundry list of *buts*. My career. The language. Money. The precarious way of life. The foreign culture. The school systems.

An ideal? Yes. Am I going? No. This is the response I give. It is also the response I have received, time and time again, in return.

I don't usually let the contradiction and inconsistency of this reply bother me. The response has enabled me to affirm my unwavering allegiance to the dream of Israel while simultaneously excusing my decision to stay here. Though we usually strive to achieve ideals, somehow we are okay with leaving the dream of aliyah respectfully untouched. Israel has become more a statement of ideology than a plan of action.

But sometimes the disingenuousness does bother me.

I recently attended the movie premier of *The Prime Ministers*, based on the book written by Yehuda Avner. Towards the end, the film described the scene of Prime Minister Golda Meir traveling up north after the bloodiest battle of the Yom Kippur War to meet her soldiers. Meir looked out over the Kuneitra Valley, dubbed the Valley of Tears, and quietly observed the silent sacrifice that had been made for a dream two thousand years old. When she asked if the soldiers had anything to ask of her, one man stood up.

"I have a question," he said. "My father was killed in the 1948 war, and we won. My uncle was killed in the 1956 war, and we won. My brother lost an arm in the 1967 war, and we won. Last week I lost my best friend over there" – he pointed to the Valley of Tears – "And we're winning. But is all our sacrifice worthwhile, Golda? What's the use of our military power if we can't win the peace?"

Eyes red, face lined with fatigue, Meir responded, "I weep for your loss, just as I grieve for all our dead. I lie awake at night thinking of them. And I must tell you, in all honesty, were our sacrifices for ourselves alone, then perhaps you are right; I'm not at all sure they would be worthwhile. But if they are for the survival of the whole Jewish people, then I believe with all my heart that any sacrifice is worthwhile."

When we think about the aliyah question, do we do so within the context of sacrifice? Israel is a country built upon sacrifice. We acknowledge and celebrate this sacrifice when it comes to others: Soldiers who gave up their lives. Friends and relatives who gave up homes, jobs, and the smaller comforts of living in the States. But when it comes to *our* jobs, our plans, our comforts, our homes, the question immediately becomes more gray. When it comes to our own lives, we hold sacrifice at arm's length – even with *"Libi ba'mizrach"* swinging around our necks and Israeli flags spotting our dorm room windows.

The inconsistency between thought and action is uncomfortable, when we pause to really consider it. We sacrifice for other ideals. Why not this one?

The movie ended. Applause. More applause. Lights went back on. Hustle towards the exits. Nods of appreciation among the almost exclusively Jewish audience – *great movie, yes. Really great.*

Then we all walked back out together to rejoin the streets of New York.

Heartbeat of the Homeland

Sarah Zadok

Sarah is a Jewish educator, content producer, and writer. She is a lover of good music, good wine, and Ba'al Shem Tov stories (in any order). She lives in the Golan Heights with her husband and their five children. Sarah made aliyah in 1999.

I'm on vacation. I'm in the U.S. on a momma-daughter bat mitzvah trip with my biggest girl. We came to celebrate her passage into young womanhood by getting seriously loved up by her grandparents, aunties, and uncles, eating obscene amounts of New York cheesecake, buying stuff, seeing some shows, and staying up late.

We're 18 hours into our vacation, and so far, I've checked on Israel's breaking news at least 10 times. I am in the lap of North American luxury – drinking freshly brewed Peet's coffee, being served scrambled eggs, and reading for leisure by an actual fireplace... I've got my Norman Rockwell *on*. But, for some reason, I am pulled by an inner force to the damn computer to read the next Israeli news bulletin, and post things to my social media account like "Wake up and smell the rocket fire, people."

I've been thinking about how every time I come to the States for a visit, something major goes down in Israel. Today for example, in Israel's news, over 20 rockets were fired into southern Israel; that's more than 110 rockets that have been fired into our country in the last 72 hours...

Please indulge me for a brief moment by pausing to let that last sentence sink in a bit...

110. Rockets. Fired. Into. Civilian. Land. In. Southern. Israel. Last. 72 hours.

In other news, in the north of Israel, the IDF returned fire into Syria after stray Syrian mortars landed on our soil just beyond our northern border. Big news indeed, as this is the first direct exchange of fire between Israeli and Syrian forces in the Golan since the Yom Kippur War.

Oh, and also, I live in the Golan Heights, about a 15-minute drive from where that mortar shell landed.

So I'm sitting here trying to figure out why something heavy always happens in Israel when I fly abroad, and then it hit me... something heavy is *always* going on in Israel... some kind of breaking, often tragic news. But here, in America, even though my news is coming from the same sources that I depend on in Israel, it just sounds way scarier.

I knew about the rocket fire in Gaza before we left. I touched base with my friends in the south, sent my love, prayed for quiet. I knew about the Syrian fire and the IDF's first response before our flight left from Brussels... I was not then, and still am not, now, concerned about my family's safety. I have every bit of faith in G-d and our holy IDF that we (the *royal* we) will be fine and ultimately safe and unaffected. But somehow, here, in the comfort of my mother's home, I am still feeling deeply unsettled.

There is a feeling of helplessness sitting on the other side of a screen, oceans between me and the place that my heart lives, waiting for information about the place that my heart lives. That's just vulnerable, and I hate feeling vulnerable.

Just last week, I was glued to CNN reading about the devastation that was ravishing the east coast of the United States, the other place that my heart lives, my mother's home. Blessedly, my mother's New Jersey home was ultimately fine, but Norman Rockwell did not live here for the last two weeks running. My family was without electricity for nine days. Although I received word on their safety, I was on *shpilkes* until her lights and heat came back on.

That's the thing about mothers' hearts – they tend to beat louder and develop arrhythmia when there is bad news amuck. There is simply something about being home that gives the heart a baseline to return to when things get a little funky; a pacemaker, if you will.

See, when I'm at home in Israel, it's not that I am doing a whole lot more than I am doing now to contribute to Israeli's political landscape. I try to stay plugged in, promote positive Israeli PR whenever possible, and occasionally opine online about it. But, mostly, I'm just home, doing my thing. At 6:30 a.m. I pack my kids their lunches, kiss their sweet freckled cheeks, and send them off to school.

But as humdrum as it may be to pack lunches and kiss cheeks, there is a deep sense of purpose in that. Those bellies fed and bodies loved are essential pixels in the greater portrait of Israel.

I guess the pixels are harder to see when I'm there, inside of it, living it, smelling it, brown paper bagging it. But, here, away from home, each rocket fired, each military action committed and, yes, each Israeli cheek kissed is a pixel that comes into a much sharper focus when I see it from a distance.

I am aware that this view from abroad is really a blessing, a gift to be able to feel so much, to feel so connected.

But I am also clear on this: I'd rather be living the news in my homeland, than reading about it from somewhere else.

I Don't Want to Go
Back to Israel

Chaya Lester

Chaya is a Jerusalem-based spiritual teacher and guide, psychotherapist, and performance artist. She is co-director of the Shalev Center for Jewish Personal Growth, where she trains and facilitates ongoing women's groups and teaches regular classes in the Jerusalem area and on her annual tours worldwide. Chaya also created a one-woman show, "Babel's Daughter," which is a unique synthesis of Jewish wisdom, psychology, and the arts. Chaya made aliyah in 1999.

It's August. Time of my annual reckoning. My yearly heart-break of a return to America, to the grandparents, the cousins, the aunties, the wall-to-wall carpeting, the ritual visits to Target, to Costco, to Morningstar Riblets in plastic packages that taste nostalgic like you-know-when, before I became religious and left all of this luxurious mouth-watering wonder and creature-comfort known as America, to live the epic run-on sentence of an Israeli dream.

Over the course of our great North American journey, I will cry regularly.

I will cry watching my brother play with my baby, absolutely aching with the knowledge that he won't see him again for another year and this child won't be much of a baby by then.

I will cry watching my progeny romp around crazy joyous

with their seldom-seen and wildly-adored cousins. I will wince with the knowledge that these five days will have to make up for the next 360 of distance.

I will cry when my Dad holds my daughter's tiny hand as they walk to get the morning paper, wishing this were every morning.

I will cry when I watch my mother's face darken as she stands in the kitchen, making pancakes for the grandkids as she remembers again – for the thousandth time – that they are leaving in a few short sunsets. To a land eight time zones away. A land where everything is foreign. A land with no grandma's pancakes. A land with no family over for the holidays. A land with no Sundays.

And I will ask myself why, why in the world, am I doing this again? To my mother, my father, my children. To my entire extended American clan. Why am I leaving again?

As I schlep this mythic weight over my shoulder onto yet another airplane set for that deliriously distant holy land.

So, let's just put the PR machines on pause for a moment, friends. Turn off the tape recorder, please. For a moment, I just want to be totally transparent. Just you and me and all my post-modern Zionistic complexity.

For the Truth, it seems, is a multi-layered and contradictory thing. On one layer, I am utterly devoted, committed and enthralled with every silky stitch of the fabric of my Israel reality. But there are other layers, too…

And at this moment, my weary soles are sticking strong to the layer where I just don't have it in me to schlep back to fulfill the great Israeli dream. For all its glory, this morning, I just don't want to leave.

For here, behind all the hype and hope, is a very real, very blurry-eyed sense of loss and home-sickened grief. In the dark corners of my otherwise bright historic prayer come true, I am weeping.

And I will continue to weep, bitter and quiet, as we board the plane to Tel Aviv in a few days. No one will see. The children will not know. I will not speak of this to the students visiting, to the Birthrighters, to the tourists at our glorious Jerusalem Shabbos table.

But, God as my witness, I am weeping up something tragic as I write this from the comfy familiar of my parents' living room tweeds.

The Gemara says that Israel is acquired by *yissurin*, by agonies.

And though my agonies are minor in comparison to the enormous sacrifices of so many others, I still ache with my own unique and bottomless bleed.

So please God, behold these two dripping handfuls of my *yissurin* as I prepare to leave. For these tears are as real as any choice bull set upon the altar in the Temple.

This wince of homesickness is my very finest offering.

Accept it, please, in all its pungent agony as I depart again from the place my bones best know as home.

And if You don't take it as a worthy offering, then, by all means, turn Your eyes to my mother's trove of *yissurin*. I have seen her hide away far too many tears and bite her tongue each time we step on that departing plane.

That woman's pain is far more weighty and worthy than mine. See her, God, as she stands and waves bewildered and shattered at the airport as we take our kids and leave.

See how she hoists up the sacrifice of her own bent and splintered hopes of a close-knit family. There it burns atop the altar of the Land of Israel won by a grandparent's *yissurin*.

So this one's in honor of her and all the grandmothers whose beloved grandchildren have been spirited away by a colossal national-religious Jewish dream.

This one's in honor of my father and his relentless commitment to my living my own dreams, even at the expense of his own grandfatherly fulfillment.

This one's in honor of all that is given up on the other side of those great big Nefesh B'Nefesh chartered planes.

It's in honor of all the grandma's pancakes that will never be tasted, never made.

All those soccer games gone unwitnessed, uncheered for and way too far away.

This one's for all those missed trips to the zoo that are the birthright of every grandparent who has ever loved their grandkid.

I acknowledge it loud and clear, dear parents. I and Israel, together we have snatched untold hopes out from under your feet.

And you, you never signed up for this mission I have so single-mindedly claimed. You are just watching from the sidelines of history with the agony that only a grandparent aching for their grandbabies can claim.

Please, forgive me. And know that I weep bitter over it with you, too.

My Israel, my aliyah, is your sacrifice.

You are the reluctant pilgrims caught up in some mysterious and historic current of Jewish destiny. Weeping bitterly with your own Israel-winning *yissurin*.

They say that we wept by the rivers of Babylon on our way out of our homeland.

No one told us that we'd also weep on the way back in.

Aliyah – Take Three

Hadassah Sabo Milner

Hadassah is a Welsh Jew who lives in Monsey, NY. She is a writer, blogger, and lifelong foodie who works as a paralegal. She's married with four sons who provide her with much fodder for her writing projects.

Thirty days from now (and 22 hours and 45 minutes) the Nefesh B'Nefesh aliyah flight will depart from JFK. My third son, Avraham, will be on that plane, winging his way to a new future. His two older brothers already live in Israel, both serving in the IDF – big footsteps to follow in, but Avraham is totally up to the challenge. I will be the proudest mother ever, with three IDF soldier sons!

Generally, the more times you do something, the easier it gets. Not completely true with sending a kid one-way to Israel. By the time Avraham gets on that plane, he will be my third child in three years to say goodbye. Yes, by now I know what's necessary for him to schlep, and what can be bought there. I know which accessories he will need for his army gun in the future, and which tactical gloves and kneepads to buy. (Buying most of that gear in triplicate these days...) The practicalities are not as daunting as they were for the first aliyah.

But, emotionally, I think it gets harder with each child. Right now, half of my kids live in Israel, and half here with me in New York. As of August 16th, the majority of my children will be 6,000 miles away. I will be even more dependent on technology to keep in touch with my progeny. While the youngest, left behind for now, is thrilled as it means he gets 100% of my attention 100% of the time (watch how quickly that'll get old for him), this mama knows she will always be calculating time changes and schedules and have her heart split between two countries – more than it has ever been.

This aliyah is harder than the others – a few weeks ago, Avraham had a nasty accident at work. In a nutshell, he broke his face, necessitating surgery and stitches, and lots of pain and suffering. Being able to be here for him, to take care of him, to make sure he got the care he needed, that he saw the right doctors, and followed the treatment plans was a blessing. I kept thinking, what if this had happened in Israel? I wouldn't be there, I wouldn't know how to navigate the healthcare system once my hastily grabbed flight to Israel would have arrived, and my time taking care of him would be finite as life back home would be calling.

I had wanted to spend some one-on-one time with him before he left, but not like this. And right now, even though he is doing so much better and his aliyah is proceeding on time, I just want to wrap him up in bubble wrap and keep him here, safe and sound. Not practical, and totally selfish. He needs to spread his wings and start living his own life. I just wish Israel wasn't so far away.

By the time August 16 rolls around, his accident will be just a memory, and we will be focused on the future. I will cry many tears as we say goodbye. There will be tears of sadness, for sure – my son is leaving home and officially beginning life as an adult – but mostly they will be tears of pride. You would think that the pride would get old, that one would get used to the idea of having one's sons move to Israel to live and to join the IDF, but every time I think about it, my heart wants to burst through my chest. My boys have made such a huge decision to move to Israel, to serve in the army, and they do it because they see that this is the right choice, the right place for them to be. I am blown away by the depth of feeling and commitment that these precious boys have found within themselves. Just thinking of that moment when he looks back and waves as he goes through passport control and out of our line of sight, I tear up. I can already see his face – a little fear, for sure, but mostly excitement and joy for what awaits him – how could I not be proud?

Avraham – be strong, my son, walk confidently towards your future – we are all so very proud of you.

The Spirituality of Jewish Geography

Akiva Gersh

Sense of place. It's a concept in the world of ecology that I was introduced to when I was 19 years old and studying environmental studies in college. At the time, I really had no idea what it meant. Even as professors and other students explained the idea to me, I found it very hard to relate to. What did it mean to feel connected to a specific place? Though I had lived in the same town for the first 17 years of my life, I felt no sense that that place, or any place, was truly *my* place.

This idea didn't begin to make sense to me until I was 22 years old, when I traveled to Israel for the first time. I had spent the previous two months traveling in West Africa, and recorded my experiences there on 13 rolls of film (remember pre-digital camera days?) and on the pages of three entire journals. My African friends wondered why I was always writing. Upon arriving in Israel, however, something strange happened. Even though it was also my first time in Israel, I suddenly found myself no longer taking pictures and no longer writing in my journal. At first, I couldn't figure out why, until one day, it hit me.

At home in New York, I didn't take pictures and I didn't write in my journal because it was home. I didn't need to. These were things I only did to document time spent in new and foreign lands. But, while Israel was in so many ways new and foreign to me, I didn't feel the need to document my daily experiences, because I felt something there that I had never felt before, not even at "home" in New York. For the first time in my life, I felt a sense of belonging. For the first time in my life, I felt a sense of place.

While I'm not the only one to experience this phenomenon, the question still begs to be asked: How is it possible that a new land felt more like home within a few days than my hometown in America ever did in almost 20 years?

To begin answering this question, I have to share a little background. I teach Jewish History at the Alexander Muss High School in Israel program in Hod HaSharon. Each group I teach begins its studies at the very beginning of the Jewish story, as we learn about our patriarch Avraham. In class, we talk about him as a man who was completely alone in his beliefs; an individual going against the grain of an entire society. Then, finally, at the age of 75, he hears his first confirming voice from the one G-d in whom he's believed courageously his entire life. But G-d doesn't open up the conversation with a simple introduction like, "Hi, my name's G-d. Thanks for believing in me!" Instead his first words to Avraham instruct him to pack his bags and get out of town. And to where? To "a *place* that I will show you."

We're not given access to Avraham's mind or thoughts at this point in the story; we're just told that he obediently leaves with his wife Sarah and a following of disciples and students. At this point in my lesson, I pause and ask my students, "What do you imagine Avraham was thinking when he heard these words? What do you think he was expecting to see in this new land to which he was being led?" All kinds of answers are shared, but, eventually, someone says that Avraham is probably expecting to be brought to a paradise-like land with people who, like him, are all monotheistic and where he can finally fit in and feel at home, no longer society's outcast and renegade. With that in mind, we continue to learn, using the text along with historical and archaeological evidence as our guides, and we see that the new land that Avraham is led to is no haven for monotheism but rather a land of idol worshippers even worse than the one he left behind.

Having discovered this, we then ask the question: Why?! Why would G-d bring Avraham, his faithful, chosen servant, to a land that is filled with moral and spiritual challenges? Why not bring him to a different land, a far-away land, even an uninhabited land, where Avraham the individual can grow into a purely monotheistic nation, removed from any tension or conflict with cultures that subscribe to opposing belief systems?

As we begin to answer this question, I share with my class an idea that I borrowed from a fellow teacher at my school: Maybe there are life lessons that Avraham, and eventually the entire Jewish people, needed to learn and things that he needed to do that could only be learned and only be done in the actual land of Israel. Maybe there's something about this place and this location that is so inherently vital to who we Jews are as a people and to our global mission, that no other land in the world could possibly do.

If we assume that is true (and I do), so what is it? What is the connection between the geographical location of the land of Israel and the vision and the mission of the nation of Israel?

There are many ways to answer this question, and here is one: When one looks at a map of the ancient world, the land of Israel stands out as hovering right in the middle between the two major civilizations of that time period, Egypt and Mesopotamia, with the major trade routes between them passing right through it. Those roads were a conduit not only for merchants from these neighboring cultures, but also for the ideas and beliefs that made them so different from Avraham and his nascent tribe. This posed both a challenge as well as an opportunity to him and, later on, to his descendants after they first settled the land. The challenge clearly was the influence of foreign traditions that could, and eventually would, sway the Jews away from their own distinct beliefs, practices, and goals. The opportunity, on the other hand, was the chance for them to positively influence the surrounding peoples with their unique approach to morals and religion, thereby allowing Avraham and his descendants to fulfill their role as "a light unto the nations."

What is so unique about the beginning of Jewish history is that our national mission, or opportunity, is born out of the very situation that creates our greatest national challenge. In fact, they intertwine in such a way as to suggest that one cannot even exist without the other, and that Judaism and the Jewish nation came into existence solely to be a literal counter-culture to the status quo. But, truth be told, this same challenge of polytheism certainly existed in Babylonia, Avraham's homeland, as did the opportunity to influence the masses with his revolutionary ideas, being that he was living in Haran, a major urban center in the ancient world.

So the question still begs to be asked: Why was Avraham sent specifically to the land of Israel to start a new nation and a new spiritual path? On one level, perhaps if Avraham was relocated to that faraway utopian society that he may have dreamed of, there would be no one to hear his message. But at the same time, staying in Haran was not an option, because, though it was his birthplace, it wasn't his *true* place in the world. He needed to be within the borders of the land of Israel to really come into the person who he truly was and was destined to be. But still the question remains! Why??

Maybe there's no perfect answer to this question. And if

there is, it's certainly not rational. It's not something that science can explain with numbers and measurements and theories. On some level, it remains deeply mysterious. But what we do know is that Avraham needed to come to Israel in order to bind himself and his descendants, the future Jewish nation, to the unique spiritual, metaphysical reality that was specially embedded in the land of Israel, in order to foster the work that he and we were specifically charged with doing in this world.

And the same can be said once again for the Jewish people today.

Jews throughout the centuries who endured the long and cruel exile envisioned the eventual return of the Jews to the land of Israel in a utopian, messianic way, with Jews flocking home from the four corners of the Earth "on the wings of eagles." Like Avraham, perhaps, they never imagined that living in Israel would be plagued with constant challenges and obstacles. And yet it was. Since returning and reestablishing ourselves on our ancient soil, we have faced decades of war, terrorism, international condemnation, and delegitimization. Could my great-grandfather from Poland ever have imagined Jews back in the land of Israel dealing with Hamas and Hezbollah? With apartheid allegations and BDS?

And the same question that we ask of Avraham we can ask of ourselves today. Namely, why did we need to come back to this specific place? Why didn't the early Zionist leaders choose to reestablish Jewish sovereignty elsewhere in the world, somewhere off to the side and out of the way? Some of those early leaders surely sensed that our presence in the Middle East would lead to years of war and conflict, yet they still moved forward with the Zionist plan, even turning down the British offer to create a Jewish state elsewhere. Why?

Just as the question is the same, the answer is as well. As

Jews, we needed to return not only to self-rule and statehood but also to the actual, physical land of Israel. To reconnect not only to the place where our ancient history happened, but, maybe more importantly, to the place where our most meaningful and significant present and future can happen, based on the intimate relationship we have with this land since the times of Avraham. Israel is the only piece of Earth in the entire world where the Jewish nation could truly be reborn; could realize and manifest its national mission, sharing with the world a universal message that echoes the words of its ancient prophets.

I write these words from New York where I'm on a family visit, staying for three weeks in the same house and in the same town where I grew up. Whenever I visit here, after the immediate culture shock wears off somewhat, I am hit with a strong sense of nostalgia for the past I had here, bordering on a longing for what I left behind when I made aliyah nine years ago. Though my love for Israel has only grown stronger with each year that I live there, when I visit America, especially when I see so many Jews living what seems like fulfilling Jewish lives here, there is a voice inside of me that bubbles to the surface and asks the question: "So, why exactly did I feel the need to move halfway across the world, far away from my family and everything I've ever known?"

On some level, life is easier here in America. Good jobs with good pay. Big green lawns for your kids to play on. Rain storms in the summer. Giant stores with everything you need (and don't need) in one place. A place where I can actually understand everything I hear on the radio and read about in the newspaper. And, to top it off, no countries or terrorist groups standing on your borders threatening your existence and reminding you daily of their desire to destroy you.

But despite my lower salary and the gas masks that sit patiently in my house, I consciously chose to live in Israel and continue to consciously choose to live in Israel. Not only live, but cling to Israel with all of my heart and soul. While it may be just another place on the map to most people in the world, it's my place, my people's place. And the only place in this great big world where I found my sense of place.

OII (Only in Israel)

Death, Israel Style

Catriella Freedman

Catriella is Director of PJ Our Way, a book-based Jewish educational program from the Harold Grinspoon Foundation. She is the author of *Foundations of Jewish Family Living*, the Melton curriculum for parents, and *My Family Story*, the middle-grade heritage program from Beit Hatfutsot. Catriella has a BA from Princeton University, an MA from Harvard University, and was a fellow at the Drisha Institute. She has lectured widely on subjects ranging from medieval Hebrew to Jewish peoplehood. She lives in Zichron Ya'akov, Israel, with Daniel, four kids, and Miles the dog. Catriella made aliyah in 2008.

I wasn't surprised, but I also wasn't prepared. After living in Israel for 10 years, you get used to everything being served raw without much subtlety. This is terrorism. This is childbirth. This is the supermarket on Erev Yom Kippur. This is recess in your child's elementary school. This is the evacuation of a settlement.

And then, this is my mother, dead. Eight months after she moved to Israel, to Zichron Ya'akov, to the same city where she had dated my father more than 62 years before.

The 5'9" woman who towered over me most of my life was now shrunken to the size of a small child, with nothing but a thin, form-fitting shroud wrapped in such a way so that I could make out the shape of her nose, her face, her arms. Like everything else, the Israeli shroud seems to say, Diaspora Jewry's simple pine box will not do; it glosses over reality. One must face the facts.

And this is my father, wracked with grief, crying and crying out with abandon. I don't remember him ever crying, but 60 years of being in America, all that learned westernization is wiped away in a cemetery in Israel, and he is finally returning to his Middle Eastern roots. He doesn't realize that I've seen this identical image before, eight years ago, when his brother with the same face buried his wife, the love of his life, in Petach Tikvah. That brother died seven years later, they say of a broken heart.

Into the earth she goes. Unceremoniously lowered in, cement bag-sized buckets of dirt are thrown in after her.

She died at nine in the morning, the silence in her hospital room the first sign that things were different. The monitors quiet, the sun streaming in, she was lying there as though napping, still warm, or was it the sun? The reaction of the staff was the second sign. Always on the move, never much time to talk or confer, nurses, doctors, orderlies, always a racing streak of white, green, and blue.

Suddenly, they appeared. One by one, they stopped, they gave hugs, they cried. For once, they didn't tell us to leave the room. I guess it didn't matter anymore. The physical therapist that had helped her with her breathing had tears streaming down her face. Doctors who never had time to talk now came. The beautiful nurse with the perfectly white hijab insisted we keep drinking, forcing cups of water into our hands. And finally, Ra'ad, the Arab nurse who had become our ally and our friend, appeared at 12 and said, you must take your father, you must get ready for the funeral. I promise you, I will not leave her side until the *Chevre Kadisha* comes to take her. I will not leave her. *Rak b'smachot*, he added, next time let us meet at a joyous occasion.

And then there was the cemetery. So many people. They had dropped everything, work, family, school, they had driven, taken buses, walked. They had come from Ashdod, Jerusalem, Bnei Brak, Ra'anana, with little more than two-hours warning, they arrived on time to witness the shrouded body and the heartbroken husband. Family, friends, many who knew my mom, many who didn't. My children's classmates, even 8-year-olds showed up to stand by my youngest daughter.

I wasn't surprised, but I also wasn't prepared for how seriously Israelis take the shiva period. A steady stream of people bearing food, stories, large ears for listening, and an ability to stay, stay, stay. Secular men arrived with kippot. Non-religious joined in the constant *minyanim*. Haredim melded with non-Haredim. It all seemed like a well-orchestrated opera; everyone knows it will be dramatic, and yet everyone knows their part.

Death creates a chasm between the living and the mystery of life. To the mourner, it feels as though that mystery will never be regained, will never be felt again. Israelis, from hard-earned experience, understand this. It seems that, as a nation, they are determined to carry each mourner back to the other side.

Only In Israel

Akiva Gersh

The first time I traveled to Israel, I was 22 years old, a year out of college, and my goals were simple. After backpacking around the country for two months, I wanted to check out life on a kibbutz and learn a bit of Hebrew. After that, my big life plan was to return to America, go back to work, eventually get married, and create another generation of Jews living in the New York section of the Diaspora.

In the end, I found a kibbutz, but I didn't last long there. In fact, I left after just three days. My thirsting soul quickly realized that it had its own agenda in Israel that the kibbutz simply could not fulfill. On a day off, I took a trip up a nearby mountain and discovered the nearby mystical city of Tzfat. I knew that was where I needed to be. I returned to the kibbutz, grabbed my backpack and traveled back up the mountain. I called Tzfat my home for the next six months, dedicating that time to exploring my Jewish roots for the first time in my life.

I did eventually return to the States, but my entire outlook on life had changed. I got a job and did things that made it seem like I was starting a career and planting my roots in America, but much of my mental energy was focused on figuring out how and when I could get back to Israel. Over the next few years, all my extra time and money went towards returning, for one week, for two weeks, for an entire summer; whatever I could manage. I never had any specific plans during these visits. Just being inside the borders of the country was enough for me. It gave me that chance to reconnect, to recharge, to refuel for the next round of life in the New York section of the Diaspora.

No matter the length of the visit, every time I came back to Israel, I felt a deep sense of being home. And with each trip I became more and more attuned to the fact that something incredibly unique was happening here. There were these moments, these experiences that kept happening all around me that I had never seen before living in America.

Beyond the obvious things like entire cities shutting down for Shabbat, Israeli soldiers everywhere walking around with M-16s on their backs and Na Nach hasidim dancing openly in the streets, there were other kinds of moments, too. Sometimes insanely funny, sometimes completely crazy, sometimes so beautiful and sweet and, yes, sometimes totally frustrating. But what they all had in common was that they happened "Only in Israel."

Like the challah you get, instead of the expected newspaper, as a bonus for filling up a full tank of gas on a Friday. Only in Israel. Or the bus that has a sticker on it that says, "This bus has already been cleaned for Pesach. Please keep it clean." Only in Israel. The woman who hands you her child to hold in the line at the grocery store because she forgot to pick up toilet paper? Only in Israel. Or how about the Arab and Jewish men praying their afternoon prayers just meters from one another in the park? Once again . . . Only in Israel.

Even if we olim were unable to articulate it before making aliyah, these moments are the reasons we moved our lives and our futures to Israel. They are also the reason we stay. These "Only in Israel" moments, the spectacular result of millions of Jews living together in the Jewish state in the Jewish homeland for the first time in 2000 years, give us a charge when our batteries run low, remind us why we came here when we begin to forget, and help us to see the big picture when we get too caught up in the minutiae of everyday life.

So, in honor of these moments and the people who make them happen, I present this collection of my favorite "Only in Israel" moments (OII for short) that I've compiled with help from fellow olim. Giggle. Laugh. Tear up. But most of all, take pleasure and feel pride in those things that happen "Only in Israel".

RELIGIOUS LIFE

I called a restaurant to place an order for take-away. In the middle of my order over the phone, I was asked to wait a few minutes as they were lighting Hanukkah candles. I heard the whole thing over the phone!

I was taking the Torah back after Shabbat morning prayers to where I could lock it up and was walking up a narrow road, when a car came toward me slowly. When it got to me, it slowed almost to a halt, the back window came down and a man in the back seat reached out, kissed the Torah, and wished me "Shabbat Shalom!"

A woman's car broke down in the middle of a traffic circle on my way home from the beach. I pulled over and helped her get it to the side of the road. She repaid me with a homemade challah.

Went to the bank today and the security guard asked me if I had a weapon. I said no and took a book of Psalms out of my pocket. He said to me, "That is a weapon!"

Only in Israel do you walk past the entrance to a shop and overhear the security guard at the door discussing the finer points of the Rambam's philosophy with another passerby.

I met a cab driver named Mashiach.

Me: Is your name actually Mashiach? Or is that a nickname?

Driver: That's actually my name.

Me: Why did your parents give you that name?

Driver: Because our family name is Ben David.

I received the following email from the Gett Taxi app right before Yom Kippur:

"Shanah Tovah, wishing you an easy fast. We apologize if we offended you in any way or G-d forbid were late to send a cab. Please note that cabs will not run on Yom Kippur."

OII does your son phone up the municipality a week before Sukkot and ask them to prune the tree in the street that overhangs our garden, because otherwise our sukkah won't be kosher. And only in Israel is the job done the next day.

The cops are called to break up a post-Simchat Torah party, but instead of breaking it up they join in the dancing.

OII do you see soldiers returning to their base during Sukkot with a gun in one hand and a *lulav* in the other.

OII do you go into a cosmetic store and the only clerk in the store is standing behind the counter praying and the several customers are patiently waiting for her to finish.

OII do kids from youth movements hand out apple slices with honey before Rosh Hashanah in city centers!

At a government tax office. I sat down at the desk of one of the workers who, upon seeing that I'm religious, made a point to tell me that that he is an atheist. He then proceeded to remove from his desk drawer a two-inch thick book filled with original insights into the weekly Torah portion that he wrote.

OII do you open the radio at 6:00 a.m. and hear *Shema Yisrael* being recited on a government station.

OII does the DJ on the radio ask people to call in to express their "*slichot*" (apologies) to the people in their lives during Rosh Hashanah time.

Our rental lease has a clause that only appears in an Israeli document. It claims we have 60 days to vacate the premises "when the *Mashiach* (Messiah) comes."

OII does the huge greasy garage door at the mechanic have a mezuzah on it.

OII does a teenager with spiked hair and torn jeans, walking down Ben Yehuda Street in Jeruslaem with his posse of friends, stop at the Chabad stand to put on tefillin.

OII does the ATM machine wish me "Mazal Tov!" on my Hebrew birthday.

OII does the hassidic community in Haifa find out that their Shabbos goy for years is actually Jewish.

OII does the guy who owns a very non-kosher deli, when asked, "How are you?" replies, "I'm good, *Baruch Hashem*," and wishes you a Shabbat Shalom.

OII are the holes in the windows at the post office that enable you to speak to the clerk in the shape of a Star of David.

OII do you get stopped on your way into a mall and asked to help make a minyan, and then find out there is even a shul there.

OII does a security guard not let you through the gate on Friday afternoon until you have told him a d'var Torah that he can repeat at Shabbat dinner.

OII can you hear *Eicha* read on the radio on Tisha B'Av.

OII, at gas stations on Fridays, instead of the usual newspaper or cup of coffee, you get a challah with a fill-up!

OII does the government building give the day off to workers who are *kohanim* when the body of Yitzchak Shamir is lying in state.

OII does the school security guard direct traffic while wearing tallit and tefillin.

OII do you get a nose-piercing done in a store called "Tattoo" with a huge picture of the Lubavitcher Rebbe at the entrance.

OII does a cop pull up next to you to tell you that you ran a red light and that you could have been hit by oncoming traffic, so you should say *"Birkat HaGomel"* (the blessing one makes after being saved from a dangerous situation).

OII do you see a woman power-walking and saying Tehillim at the same time.

OII are you in basic training during Sukkot and get challenged by your commander to build a proper succah, and if you don't, you have to do push-ups.

OII do you hear the *Shecheyanu* prayer (thanking God) being recited by the guy who is informed on the radio that he has won the lottery.

OII do kids go to school on December 25th and have no idea what the day means to most of the world.

OII, do you hear someone at a McDonald's in Tel Aviv say:

"Hi, is the bread kosher for Passover?"

"Yes, of course."

"Great, then I'll take a cheeseburger and a strawberry milkshake."

Living in the Middle East

OII does my local health food store carry only one brand of peanut butter, but more than fifteen varieties of tahini, and only one brand of maple syrup, but ten brands of date syrup.

That moment in Ramle when a group of IDF soldiers is waiting for the train and one offers his comrades a bite of ice cream, and one of the guys says, "I can't, I'm fasting since it's Ramadan." And then another one says, "Yeah, me neither. I ate meat for lunch, so I can't eat dairy for another two hours."

We scheduled for an exterminator to come to our house. We left a key and payment for his services in a Ziploc bag because we weren't going to be at the house at the time we scheduled. We got a call from him upon his arrival asking if he could keep the Ziploc! Apparently he'd never seen such a nice bag!

OII does the Muslim cashier at my local supermarket wear Minnie Mouse ears over her hijab for Purim.

OII do you see a man guiding a herd of sheep with one hand and using his cell phone in the other.

OII can your six-year-old daughter explain the Israeli-Arab conflict, doing an incredible job covering the essential points.

OII do you see an ultra-Orthodox woman school an Arab teen in Jerusalem about the dangers of smoking. "Are you crazy?" she said. "Are you trying to kill yourself? Take a deep breath and see how sweet the air is when you put down your cigarette." He put out his cigarette and thanked her.

An OII moment at Hebrew University: As a Jewish student comes out of his classical Arabic class, an Arab student rushes past, shouting out to her Arab friend, "Which class are you running to, Jews in the Middle Ages?" To which her friend responds, "No! Hassidut!"

OII do you see Arab workers at a hotel eating matzah brei on Pesach.

Two elderly men got on the light rail in Jerusalem and started to argue about who is more entitled to the one remaining available seat. One said he lost all of his friends fighting in the Yom Kippur War and he ended up wounded and requiring a cane to walk. The other countered that he was injured in a terror attack in the First Intifada and also required a cane to walk. Upon hearing their stories, a young man stood up and gave up his seat so that both men could sit. By that point, the door opened up at the next station and an old Muslim woman stepped inside covered head to toe in a burka. Both crippled elderly Jewish men stood up with their canes and offered the Arab woman their seat.

My friend's son was in the army dining hall during Pesach. He went to get some matzah. When the soldier giving out the matzah saw his kippah, he asked if he would like some hand-shmurah matzah. My friend's son was quite happy to accept and went back to his table with a round matzah and a smile. A Bedouin soldier at his table said, "What? How did you get that?" My friend's son said, "The guy assumed that since I have a kippah I would prefer it." The Bedouin said "What? It's only for the Jews?" The next thing he knew the Bedouin soldier takes my friend's son's kippah, plunked it on his own head and went to get matzah. My friend's son called out, "It won't work!" but a minute later Mohammed returned with a round matzah and a big smile on his face – and gave my friend's son back his kippah.

OII do the stores sell Christmas lights as Sukkot decorations, and the average Israeli is clueless.

SECURITY

OII does your four-year-old explain, totally matter-of-factly, that the kids with the daddies who are fighting in the war right now are the ones who get to sit next to the teacher during story time.

When there was a war going on in the middle of my exam period at university, the exam instructions were: "Please write with a black or blue pen. No additional material allowed. In case of a siren, turn your exam paper upside down and go to the nearest shelter."

My kids were using magnetic blocks to build a house, and suddenly one of them shouted, "Oh no! We forgot to build a bomb shelter!" The next hour was spent deciding where in the house to put the shelter and how to make its walls and ceiling strong enough to survive any missiles.

OII do they have a security exercise in our community that includes the army, fire department, ambulance and local police, but only after they start do they send out reassuring emails that nothing is wrong .

OII does a radio station announce that a couple due to get married tonight in Beersheva is looking for an alternative wedding location in the Jerusalem area because of the threat of rocket attacks, and if any halls are available today at a few hours' notice, they should call the radio station.

OII do we warn our enemies before we attack.

OII does a rocket attack warning go off on Friday afternoon and people think that it is the siren announcing the start of Shabbat.

OII does the female radio broadcaster explain in a calm, sexy voice how to react if you're driving when you hear the siren: "Carefully drive to the side of the road, get out of your car, and find somewhere safe to hide. Or, if you don't have time, lie on the ground away from your car and put your hands over your head." After that announcement, halfway through the song "Stairway to Heaven", she announces, again in a calm and sexy voice, "Red Alert in Ashkelon," "Red Alert in Ashdod."

OII are the two news captions "Ceasefire is in effect" and "Air raid alert in Ashkelon" on the screen at the same time, one below the other.

OII would you combine picking up gas masks at the distribution point in the local shopping mall with buying school supplies.

I was listening to the Army radio station on Yom HaZikaron. They're sharing story after story about soldiers who have died in Israel's wars. They take a quick break for a traffic report, except that the traffic lady (probably around 20 years old) is not ready, and has to clear her throat, apologizing – she's been listening to the program, too, and is crying.

OII does a driver who parked his car illegally put his phone number inside the window along with a note that says, "Went to my brother's grave."

HUMOROUS

OII will you see someone on the train pull out a full-on electrical power strip from their bag so that they can charge their phone, laptop, and tablet all at the same time.

While wandering through IKEA, most of the model kitchens have scattered photos of random Swedish families. One kitchen has photos of a Haredi family, a prayer book on a shelf, and two sinks labeled "meat" and "milk."

From the window of the bus I was on, I saw a man in his pajamas, holding a gun, waiting at a bus stop. I thought to myself, "If this guy gets on the bus, I'm getting off." The bus stopped at the bus stop and a female soldier got off, greeted the man in the pajamas, and then took the gun from him. Apparently, the man was her father bringing the gun she had forgotten at home!

OII have I seen a beggar rattling her cup with one hand and talking on a cell phone held in her other hand.

You're on a public bus and people start to realize that the driver has veered from the regular route. Turns out that he made a detour to his home to collect the sandwiches that he forgot there.

OII does your bus driver reply he has no time to read at home when you ask him not to read while he is driving.

OII do you call a company to make an order and the employee who answers tells you that he is on the phone with a friend, that your 300 shekel order isn't worth hanging up for, and then says goodbye.

Just had a guy come to my front door looking for a different address and argue with me that he was in the right place.

OII does the nurse at the doctor's office tell my husband, "Your little girl looks exactly like you. It's a pity, since you have such a beautiful wife."

OII did a guy take the opportunity to try and ask me out while we were hiding in a bomb shelter during an air raid siren in Tel Aviv.

OII does a woman ask you if she can borrow your phone quickly (while you're using it). You give it to her, and she continues to have a 10 minute conversation on it. When you tell her your bus is coming and you need your phone back, she tells you, "It's ok, I'm taking the same bus."

OII can you be the first person at the bus stop but the last one to actually get onto the bus.

OII can you go to a belly dancing class where half of the students are young Arab women from nearby villages, and the class is being taught by a Russian woman speaking Hebrew.

OII can you pass over three lanes of traffic with no blinker in the middle of an intersection and not get pulled over by the traffic cop who is driving right behind you.

OII do you see a guy give money to a beggar and then ask him for change because he didn't have anything smaller on him.

OII would a woman absorbed in reading her book at a bus station look up and say loudly, "When the 91 bus comes, somebody tell me!"

I was lost in Tel Aviv and needed to get to Beit Hillel Street. I was actually standing on Beit Hillel, but just didn't know it. I asked five different people for directions and got five different answers, most of which would have had me walking many blocks out of my way. Not a single person admitted that they just didn't know.

OII do the taxi drivers get insulted when you put on your seat belt.

OII do grown men in business attire eat ice cream on a stick while trying to close a deal in a meeting.

We went out to dinner with friends one night and decided to check out a new restaurant.

"What's the difference between the two seating sections?" our friend asked the maître d'.

"In this section, smoking is not allowed," he answered, indicating the section we were seated in. Then he thought about it for a moment, and added: "In that section smoking is also not allowed. But people smoke."

A bus driver from Tiberias to Tel Aviv (no short journey) says: "I've never done this route before. Here's a list of 45 stops between here and Tel Aviv, turn on your GPS on your phone, sit next to me and tell me where to go."

My friend was entering the Tel Aviv Central Bus Station when the Russian security guard noticed a long tubular thing in his backpack. "That looks like C-4 plastic explosives," he said. He then continued to shut down the entire area and call in the police. When the first policeman (a Yemenite Jew) showed up, he said, "You brought me here for that? That's frozen *jachnun* (a Yemenite pastry)!"

WE ARE FAMILY!

This morning while waiting for a bus, there were three Egged bus drivers waiting with us, one holding a bunch of flowers. They got on the bus after us and announced that the driver of the bus was retiring after many years of service with Egged. The passengers all applauded, photographs were taken, and then one of the three took over the driver's seat while the retiring driver was ushered into a car along with green and white balloons. Everyone was smiling and happy even though there had been a slight delay.

OII would a driver who gave me a lift, and whom I completely don't know, stop to go to a store during the drive and leave me in his car with the keys in the ignition!

I was at a restaurant and asked the waiter what the woman at the next table was eating, as it looked good. The woman apparently overheard me asking because she proceeded to ask the waiter for a small plate and put part of her portion on it. She then brought it over to me, saying that it is delicious and I have to try it!

OII do girls walk down the street handing out cookies for free. OII do you take one without hesitation, concern, or fear that something's wrong with them.

I walked into my garden, which is surrounded by a wall and a gate, and found a woman about 50 years old standing under my mulberry tree and eating all my mulberries. When I asked her why she was in my garden, she told me that I had too many mulberries and she didn't want them to go to waste. We stood looking at her and waiting for her to leave – but she just remained there eating!

OII does the lady behind you in line at the supermarket reach over and fussily tuck the tag down into the back of your shirt.

OII will the guy sitting in front of you on the bus, a total stranger, ask you for a sip from your water bottle. And OII do you say yes.

A 19-year-old female soldier who lives with her mom, a single parent, and earns the lowly army salary that soldiers in Israel earn, is sitting on the train on her way home. She is on the phone with the electric company, begging them not to cut off her family's electricity before her mom can receive her check from social security to repay the debt. Suddenly another passenger comes over to the soldier, takes her phone, and pays the 2000 shekel debt right from his pocket with a smile on his face.

My receipt for getting my washing machine fixed said: "Technician service: 200 shekels. For soldiers: 0." It went on to say: "You take care of our security; we take care of the washing machine."

OII is the cashier on her cellphone making a *shidduch* while checking out my groceries.

A soldier at a supermarket, after the cashier rings up all of his items, discovers that there is no money on his *"choger"* (a monthly stipend for food) when he tries to pay. The checkout woman doesn't hesitate and pulls out her own credit card. When the soldier tries to stop her, she insists and tells him her brother is about to enlist soon and that this is the least she could do for our wonderful soldiers. He leaves embarrassed and grateful while she wishes him luck and tells him to keep safe.

Overheard at a supermarket in Bnei Brak:

Security guard: "Sir, you can't take the shopping cart out of the parking lot! You must leave your ID card with me!"

Man (rushing back): "Here, take my son! I'll be right back!"

A mother walks past a security guard in his booth outside of a parking lot. She has a baby in her arms. Upon seeing this, the guard gets up, puts both his hands on the baby's head, asks for the baby's full name and gives him a blessing.

There was a knock at the front door. There stood a few children, asking if my kids were at home. "No," I replied, "they went out." "Not a problem," one of the kids said, "we can play here by ourselves," and they walked right into my house.

It was a rainy day and the buses were running late. I was waiting at the bus stop for 25 minutes. My bus comes only once every half an hour. The bus finally arrived and I signaled to the bus driver to stop. Apparently, he misunderstood and thought that I didn't need that line. The bus right behind him stopped. He saw how upset I was and asked where I needed to go. I told him I wanted the previous bus. He told me not to worry, that G-d will watch over me. He then proceeded to call the driver of the bus that passed me and arranged for him to wait for me at the next stop, then dropped me off so I could make my bus.

A bride parked her ribbon-decorated car on the street when she went shopping after her wedding. She came back to find a note on her car. Thinking she had been hit, she nervously read the note to find that a stranger who didn't know her had wished her "Mazal Tov!" and left her a gift of 100 shekels.

A group of about twenty soldiers were on their way back to their base and stopped to buy some burgers. A few minutes after they ordered, the guy behind the counter let them know that a man who had just snuck out the door had paid for their entire order – and also left them 100 shekels each as a gift for Rosh Hashana!!

While waiting for my turn at the car registration office, I am approached by a young man who is on the phone with one of his suppliers. He sees that I speak English and asks me if I would talk to his supplier to try and get the price down on t-shirts he wants to buy from him. I get on the phone … and get the price down by 26 cents apiece!

Our taxi driver from the airport not only had his 4-year-old son in the car with him (it was a Friday), but also a coffee machine plugged into a power pack which he used to make us a hot, fresh cup of coffee for the ride!

While I was fighting with the cashier at the supermarket

because my card got rejected, the couple behind me paid for my groceries and told me "write us a check someday."

I was at the supermarket with my young daughter and crying baby, when a worker came over and smiled, took the baby, kissed him and then walked off with him. When I went after them to see what was going on, she told me that she thought a little walk around would calm him and make it less stressful for me.

I was in Eilat visiting my son. Half an hour after leaving to drive up north, I discovered that he had left his wallet in my bag. I stopped at the next rest stop, found someone who was driving south to Eilat, gave him the wallet and he drove out of his way to deliver it to my son.

Saturday morning, 6 a.m., my water breaks (pregnant with twins)! I go outside to hail a cab to the hospital. As we get closer, I realize I only have 10 agurot in my wallet. Stopping at an ATM seems scary since I've heard you can deliver very quickly after your water breaks. We get to the hospital. I give my ATM card to my Arab cab driver and tell him, "Here's my code, go get the money." He comes back and tells me the machine is broken. He gives me his phone number. Two days later, I call to tell him that I have his money and he says, "But wait! Did you give birth? Boy? Girl? Is everything okay? How do you feel? How are the little ones?" Only then will he talk about getting his money back!

OII does the taxi driver who brings your son to school every day bring *sufganiot* for the whole family on Hanukkah to apologize for occasionally being a little late!

One Shabbat morning, there was a knock on my door. I asked in Hebrew, "Who's there?" The answer shouted back at me: "A Jew!" I opened up the door and found a Haredi Jew standing there in full Shabbat garb. He asked me if I had any hot water I could give him. I said, "Sure," and went into my kitchen to get him some, but realized that I didn't have a disposable cup to give it to him in. He said, "Don't worry, you can use this," as he hands me a crinkled plastic cup he was holding in his hand. As I turned around to go fill it with water he added, "And if you happen to have some coffee around and could add that to the hot water, that would be great." I smiled and facetiously added, "Would you like milk with that?" He answered, taking me completely seriously, "No thanks, I don't need."

When a lady in a Jerusalem taxi realized she had left her purse at home, the taxi driver not only told her not to worry about the fare but insisted on giving her money so she'd be able to get home again later.

OII does the woman at the cash register of the mini market see the rice cakes in your bag, share the fact that rice cakes give her constipation, and then asks you if they do the same for you.

OII can your daughter, who works in Tiberias and needs to get her *teudat zehut* from home in Efrat, send it with a friend to the Central Bus Station in Jerusalem, who gives it to the bus driver on the next bus leaving to Tiberias, who then calls her when he gets there for her to meet him to come get it!

Some time ago, I had to go to the Ministry of Interior in Kfar Saba to register my change in marital status after getting divorced. After completing all the necessary paperwork, the office supervisor looked over and gave me a reassuring smile. "Don't worry… you'll find someone else", she declared. She then picked up a biscuit off the saucer next to her teacup and handed it to me. "Here, have a cookie," she said encouragingly.

OII will you ask someone for directions and get the response: "That is very far, you need to take a bus or a cab to get there." This is overheard by an elderly lady, who responds, "It is not far at all, only 15 minutes on foot," and then walks you almost all the way there.

OII will people you don't know leave their luggage with you in the airport while they walk around, and then come back with a croissant as a gift for watching their stuff.

As our overtired baby began to wail on the crowded bus, the bus driver stopped the bus and walked back to our seat. I was sure he was going to tell us off, but instead he pulled out a candy and handed it to my daughter and told her not to forget to say a blessing before eating it!

My sister and I got into a taxi in Jerusalem. Of course, upon hearing us speak English, the driver started speaking to us in English. My sister told him that Hebrew is fine since we've been living here for over 30 years. So the guy started telling us about an American woman who's a regular client. He started asking us if we know her, and it was a good thing that I controlled a snicker and held my tongue, because I was about to say, "Do you honestly think we know every American lady in Jerusalem?" His client turned out to be a good friend of my sister. We chatted a bit and got to our destination. Later on in the day, my sister discovered that an important zip pack with cash, a purse, a cable and earphones was not with her. She looked everywhere and concluded that either she lost it, or, hopefully, left it at home. As she was arriving home more than three hours after the taxi ride, she got a call from the taxi driver who had found her case. And how did he get her number? From her dear friend who happened to be his regular client!

A young female soldier got off her bus to catch her next bus and just missed it. The next bus was in five hours! As it is against army regulations to hitchhike, she prepared to nap at the bus stop until the next bus came and prayed that she would not be punished for being so late. A couple of minutes later, an older Sephardi couple stopped and offered her a ride. She thanked them profusely, but told them that she is not permitted to hitchhike. They continued to insist, so the soldier replied: "I am allowed to get rides with family, so if you act like you are my family when you drop me off at the base, then it will be okay." The couple agreed, and as they dropped her off, the "imma" got out of the car and hugged the soldier, telling her to take care of herself, that they were going to miss her, and that she must remember to call. The "abba" brought out her bag and continued on about her staying safe and of course staying in touch and remembering to call. The soldier promised to call. This was all witnessed by the soldier's commanders.

I am a soldier. I got off at the train station in Nahariya and went into a bakery. I picked out a couple of pastries, and when I went to pay, I noticed that my wallet was gone. I asked them to watch my kitbag and ran off to search for my wallet. I found it, in a trash can, emptied of the 300 shekels I had in it. I went back to the bakery and told them what happened and that I wouldn't be able to pay. They insisted that I take the bag of pastries anyway, which they continued to fill. I thanked them a lot and left. Later when I opened up the bag to eat the pastries, I found not only the pastries, but also 300 shekels in cash.

Afterword

When I begin to teach my students at the Alexander Muss High School in Israel about early Zionism, we travel to the Negev to visit, among other sites, the grave of David Ben Gurion. We sit in the shadow of his grave and discuss Ben Gurion's vision and philosophy. We talk about how he wanted all Jews from around the world to make aliyah. How he firmly believed that he and his fellow pioneers were opening up the gates and paving the way for the mass return of the Jews to Israel after 2000 years of exile. How he maintained that there was no other place in the world fitting for a Jew to live.

After giving my students the opportunity to share their reactions to Ben Gurion's ideas, I invite them to ask me questions about what it's like to actually make aliyah. To leave America behind and move one's life to Israel.

They inevitably ask me what I love about having made aliyah as well as what is challenging about it. I share with them stories similar to the ones that fill the pages of this book. Inspiring ones, ones that express what it's like to take part in the long-awaited and historic return of the Jewish people to our homeland. What it's like to live in a country that was created specifically for the Jewish nation, where Jewish holidays are the national holidays, and where our people are creating a new and vibrant culture based on ancient ideas and ideals.

And I also share with them the hard parts. Like leaving family behind. Like still feeling that I don't fit in 100% after all these years. I tell them about the days where I feel like I can't say a single thing right in Hebrew. The days that make me want to run far away from Israeli cultural norms that I never want to accept as my own.

I always end by sharing with my students something that may surprise them. I tell them that there have indeed been times when my wife and I have toyed with the idea of possibly, just possibly, returning back to America. Where we would be able to live an "easier" life, in Vermont or Maine or California. A life far away from the Middle East conflict. A life in which we would understand exactly what everyone around us is saying and we'd be able to express ourselves freely, without effort.

But, I tell them, those daydreaming, musing conversations always end in the same way for me, with the following emphatic realization:

I would never leave Israel.

But why not? Why not go back to America and simplify my life?

Of course there are all of the obvious spiritual, Jewish, and feel-good "Only in Israel" reasons. And I go through them one by one with my students.

But there's one other reason, I tell them, that overshadows them all:

My children.

It is my children that will always keep me here. No matter how hard of a day, or as the case may be, how many hard days in a row I may have, the knowledge that they are growing up in the world's one Jewish state is reason enough to stay. Knowing that my aliyah has spared them of the challenges that I have gone through, and that being Israeli is simply the only reality they know, is another. Ultimately, I have come to understand that my struggles and sacrifices are but the birth pangs of a process much larger than myself. That by making aliyah I am doing my small part in bringing the Jewish people back home, and by raising my children in Israel I have ensured that the place they feel most at home is their people's ancestral homeland.

But it's not only about them not having to struggle with Hebrew or fitting into Israeli society. More importantly, I choose Israel because of the kind of people my children are becoming here. The kind of people I now know they could never become in America or anywhere else in the world. Because Israelis are who they are because of the unique combination of circumstances that exists "Only in Israel".

I illustrate this point to my students with a personal story, and with this I will end this book of stories.

It was five years ago when my firstborn son was five years old. We were still living in Jerusalem at the time and it was a beautiful and breezy Friday afternoon. Miraculously, my wife and I were ready for Shabbat a good hour before it was set to begin and we were taking advantage of the extra time by playing with our son on the floor. And then a siren went off. I hadn't heard a siren in a very long time and my first reaction was to assume that it was an air raid siren. Within moments, though, I realized that it was the Shabbat siren that goes off every Friday afternoon 40 minutes before sunset to let people know that it's time to light the Shabbat candles. For some reason, it was our first time ever hearing it in all of our years living in Jerusalem. I remained on the floor ready to continue playing.

My son, however, had a different reaction to the siren. He immediately forgot about his toys, stood up, folded his hands behind his back and bowed his head, standing in complete silence.

You see, it was just a few weeks after Yom Hazikaron, Israel's memorial day for fallen soldiers, during which a siren is sounded, once at night and once in the morning, and the entire country, from Eilat down south up to the northern border with Lebanon, stands in complete silence. Including young schoolchildren. Including my five-year-old son.

To my son, young as he was, the sound of a siren was a signal to stop and focus, to remember and give honor to those who made the ultimate sacrifice for the State of Israel. These values sink in so deeply that even at the tender age of five, an Israeli child knows what he owes, and to whom. Recognition and gratitude are hardwired into the Israeli psyche.

Contrast this with my experience of Memorial Day in America as a kid. For me, it was a day off from school, a three-day weekend, an extra day to play with my friends. I never gave it much thought and never comprehended its deeper significance, not at age fifteen or even age twenty, and certainly not at the age of five.

As my son stood in silence with his little head bowed, I sat there crying. I looked at him and realized I was home. For if this is the kind of person Israel is shaping him into, then there is simply no other place I'd rather be.

Am. Yisrael. Chai.

About the Editor

Akiva Gersh first visited Israel in 1998 at the age of 22. Within days, he knew that he wanted to make Israel his future home; a dream he fulfilled when he made aliyah with his wife Tamar in 2004. Since 2007, he has been teaching Jewish History and Modern Israel at the Alexander Muss High School in Israel, where he guides visiting high school students through the story of the Jewish people, mainly through *tiyulim* (excursions) to historical, cultural, religious, and ecological sites around the country. He is also a contributing blogger at the Times of Israel as well as a musician. In 2010, Akiva created Holy Land Spirit, an uplifting and spiritual musical experience for Christian groups visiting Israel that fosters interfaith celebration, understanding, and dialogue. Akiva holds a BA in Religious Studies from Brown University and an MA in Jewish Education from Yeshiva University. He and his wife live in Pardes Hanna with their four children.

Made in the USA
Columbia, SC
08 December 2020